Assembly Rooms at the 199.
transferring to the Riverside Studios in London
year (revived in 2000 at the Manchester Royal Exchange).
Bluebird was produced by the Royal Court in London in
1998. Simon Stephens was Pearson Writer-in-Residence
at the Royal Exchange Theatre in 2000/1, and the Arts
Council Resident Dramatist in 2000 at the Royal Court. His
next play, *Herons* (Royal Court, 2001), was nominated for the
Olivier Award for Most Promising Playwright. His radio play
Five Letters to Elizabeth was broadcast on Radio 4 in 2001,
and *Digging* on Radio 4 in 2003. His next stage play, *Port*
(Royal Exchange, Manchester, 2002), was awarded the
Pearson Award for Best New Play in 2001/2. *One Minute*
was produced by the Actors' Touring Company, Sheffield,
in June 2003; *Christmas* premiered at the Pavilion Theatre,
Brighton, in the same year. Both plays transferred to the
Bush Theatre, London, in 2004; and *Country Music* was
produced by the Royal Court in 2004. He is currently the
Writers Tutor for the Young Writers Programme at the
Royal Court Theatre.

by the same author and available from Methuen

HERONS
PORT
ONE MINUTE
CHRISTMAS
COUNTRY MUSIC

available later in 2005

SIMON STEPHENS PLAYS 1

Simon Stephens

On the Shore of the Wide World

Methuen Drama

Published by Methuen 2005

1 3 5 7 9 10 8 6 4 2

First published in 2005 by
Methuen Publishing Limited
215 Vauxhall Bridge Road
London SW1V 1EJ

Copyright © Simon Stephens, 2005

Simon Stephens has asserted his rights under
the Copyright, Designs and Patents Act, 1988,
to be identified as the author of this work

Methuen Publishing Limited Reg. No. 3543167

A CIP catalogue record for this book is available
from the British Library

ISBN: 0 413 77517 8

Typeset by Country Setting, Kingsdown, Kent
Printed and bound in Great Britain by
Cox and Wyman Ltd, Reading, Berkshire

Caution

On the Shore of the Wide World was first presented at the Royal Exchange Theatre, Manchester, supported by the Bulldog Prinsep Theatrical Foundation, on 13 April 2005. The cast was as follows:

Peter Holmes	Nicholas Gleaves
Alice Holmes	Siobhan Finneran
Charlie Holmes	David Hargreaves
Ellen Holmes	Eileen O'Brien
Alex Holmes	Thomas Morrison
Christopher Holmes / Taxi Driver	Steven Webb
Sarah Black	Carla Henry
Paul Danziger	Matt Smith
John Robinson	Roger Morlidge
Susan Reynolds	Susannah Harker

Director	Sarah Frankcom
Designer	Liz Ascroft
Lighting	Mick Hughes
Sound	Peter Rice
Assistant Director	Tom Daley

On the Shore of the Wide World

for my wife

Characters

Peter Holmes, *thirty-nine*
Alice Holmes, *thirty-seven*
Charlie Holmes, *sixty-six*
Ellen Holmes, *sixty-two*
Alex Holmes, *eighteen*
Christopher Holmes, *fifteen*
Sarah Black, *seventeen*
Paul Danziger, *nineteen*
John Robinson, *thirty-six*
Susan Reynolds, *thirty-five*
Taxi Driver, *twenty*

The Taxi Driver must be played by the same actor who plays Christopher Holmes.

The play is set in Stockport. It takes place over a nine-month period in 2004.

The set should be as open, as uncluttered, as free from specific detail as we can get away with.

The actors should enter the stage for their first entrance in each part and remain on stage until their final line of that part. Scenes can play across any actor that remains on stage regardless of whether or not they are present within that scene.

Lights should only fall completely between each part, not between each scene

Massive thanks are due to Sarah Frankcom, Lucy Davies and all at the NT Studio, the staff and writers of the Royal Court Young Writers Programme (especially Nina), Ian Rickson for the note on the drinking, Nicholas Hytner and Braham Murray for the lunch, Mum, Mark, Jane, all the folks, both the boys, and the frankly gorgeous Mel Kenyon, without whom etc., etc., etc.

Part One

Christopher

One

Alex Holmes *and* **Sarah Black** *on the top deck of a bus bound from Manchester to Stockport. Friday morning, 1.30 a.m., February 2004.* **Alex** *is drinking from a can of Red Stripe.*

Alex Have a guess.

Sarah I can't

Alex Go on.

Sarah A million miles.

Alex Ninety-three million.

Sarah God.

Slight pause.

Sarah *thinks.* **Alex** *looks at her. Drinks from his can of beer.*

Sarah *takes out a vial of pills and pops one. He watches her.*

She grins.

Sarah You wanna go somewhere else?

Alex Where?

Sarah What time is it?

Alex Half-one.

Sarah I reckon we could find somewhere. Bound to be somewhere open.

Alex At this time?

Sarah Must be. Should just go and ask someone. Go up to them. Bet they'd tell us.

Alex   You would and all.

Slight pause.

Sarah   We should go and get some fags. I could kill a fag right now.

Alex   Shouldn't smoke on a bus. It's rude.

Sarah   Nobody minds.

Alex   Yeah they do. It's dangerous, secondary smoking. Gives yer cancer.

Sarah   Coward.

Alex   It's not about being a coward, Sarah. It's just about being polite.

Sarah   What's it like being you, eh?

Beat.

We could go to yours *tonight*.

Alex *laughs.*

Sarah   We could, though.

Alex   I don't think they'd be too happy.

Sarah   They wouldn't mind.

Alex   You don't know 'em.

Sarah   I bet they're not as bad as you make out.

Alex   They'll be asleep.

Sarah   I'd be dead quiet.

Alex   You say that now.

Sarah   I would be.

Alex   I don't think it's a very good idea.

Sarah *rubs her eye gently with her thumb.*

She clears some dust.

A slight pause.

I don't want to go home.

A slight pause.

You can see the moon.

A slight pause.

How far away's that?

Alex   238,000 miles. Practically next door.

A slight pause.

Sarah   Did you check about tomorrow, Alex?

Alex   Yeah.

Sarah   What did they say?

Alex   Said it was all right. Said you could. Said as long as you were quiet and didn't ask fucking questions about the fucking moon all night then they didn't mind.

A slight pause.

Sarah   I can't wait.

A slight pause.

What are they like?

Alex   You'll see. They're all right. Bit . . .

Sarah   What?

Alex *grins, doesn't answer.*

A slight pause.

Alex   Our Christopher wants to meet you.

Sarah   Right.

Alex   There's a place he goes to. This derelict hotel. The Bluebell. He breaks in. Smokes fags. He said he wanted me to take you there to meet him.

Sarah   Right.

Slight pause.

She smiles at him. Leans against him but looks out of the bus window.

(*Looking away.*) I can always go out on my own. If you wanna go home. Go and wander about a bit.

Alex   Don't.

Sarah (*grinning*)   Have an explore.

Alex   Sarah, don't be stupid.

Sarah   Well. Come with us then.

Alex *looks away from her. Cross.*

Sarah   You can kiss us, you know. If you want to. I won't batter you.

Alex *looks down at her. Smiles.*

Two

Peter *and* **Alice** *are in their kitchen.* **Alice** *is watching the television there. It is 6.00 p.m. on Friday. As* **Peter** *talks he circles behind her, their conversation refracted through the television.*

Peter   You wanna drink?

Alice   I'm all right.

Peter   I should put the fire on. Close the curtains, eh?

No response.

He removes some chewing gum from his breast pocket and pops it in his mouth.

Chris in?

Alice   He's upstairs.

Peter   How's his day?

Alice It was all right, he said. It was good. Said it was great. He was very enthusiastic about it.

Peter Alex back yet?

Alice Not yet.

Peter He out with Sarah?

Alice I think so.

Peter What time did he get back last night?

Alice I didn't hear.

Peter Have you met her yet?

Alice I did briefly. He stopped in to get some money. She was waiting for him.

Peter What's she like?

Alice It was hard to tell. She was quite shy. They're still at the age where we make them shy. Make them clam up. I think that they think that we actually come from the moon or something. She was quite smiley, which I liked.

Peter She pretty?

Alice She is. Yeah.

Peter It's odd, isn't it?

Alice What?

Peter Just the whole idea of them having girlfriends. I find it a bit unnerving.

Alice It scares the shit out of me.

He opens himself a small bottle of beer.

Takes his chewing gum out to drink it.

Drinks with real thirst.

Peter Did he ask about tomorrow?

Alice Not again, no.

Peter What do you think?

Alice I have no idea.

Peter No. Me neither.

Alice I think I'm scared of them being adults. I don't know if it's because I still want to protect them or because I'm frightened of getting old.

He goes to kiss the top of her head. She doesn't look round.

He's not stupid. They'll be careful. We should let her.

Peter Yeah.

Alice I'll talk to him.

Peter Okay.

Slight pause. He looks at the TV with her.

You wanna go out?

Alice I don't know if I can be bothered.

Peter We could go for a curry.

Alice We could do.

Peter (*looking at her*) Or a Chinese. Could go into town.

Alice It's a bit far.

Peter We could do. I'd drive.

Alice I'm a bit tired.

Peter We've not been for a Chinese for ages, eh?

Alice No.

Peter Bit of Dim Sum. Bit of Won Ton soup.

Alice Peter.

Peter Spare-fucking-ribs and a Tsing Dao.

Alice I'm tired.

Peter Seaweed.

Alice   I'm tired, Peter.

Peter   Okay.

Alice   I don't really want to.

Peter   It's okay. It's not a big deal.

Alice   I just want to watch the telly or something.

Peter   It was just an idea, love. We can stay in. I'll cook.

Alice   We could get a take-out.

Peter   I'll cook for you. What do you fancy? What have we got in the fridge?

Alice   I think there's some tuna.

Peter   I'll cook you a tuna. How's that?

Alice   That's lovely. That'd be lovely.

A slight pause.

Peter   Do we need to cook for Sarah, do you think?

Alice   I don't know. I'm not entirely sure that they actually eat any more.

Three

Charlie *and* **Ellen**'s *house. Their living room.* **Charlie** *and* **Ellen** *have returned home from a funeral reception. It is Friday, 7.00 p.m. They are removing their coats.*

Ellen   I don't feel like cooking.

Charlie   No.

Ellen   You could go to the chip shop if you were hungry.

Charlie   I'm full. Of ham sandwiches.

Ellen   I thought she was very brave.

Charlie   Yes.

Ellen   It probably won't hit her for a bit. That's what happens, isn't it?

Charlie   I think it varies. From person to person.

Ellen   I don't know how I'd cope. I don't know how I'd bear it.

Charlie   I think you probably would. You kind of just do, I suspect.

Ellen   I always thought Angus Morsten was a very odd name. Are you all right?

Charlie   I am. Yes.

Ellen   You should have gone to see him, you know.

Charlie   I know.

Ellen   You'll regret that, I bet.

Charlie   Too late now, Ellen.

She brings him a gin and tonic. She has a vodka and tonic.

Ellen   They should have had a singer. I think I'd like a singer. There's something sterile about a compact disc. The thing I always think about is going back to the house again. Afterwards. You walk in the door and I think probably all the furniture and the carpets and everything you've got must look different. You miss the smell, I bet. The sound of somebody moving around the house. Waking up in the night and having the feel of somebody lying there. Are you sure you're all right, really?

Charlie   I think so.

Ellen   You can tell me, you know?

Charlie   I'm fine.

Ellen   Put the television on.

Charlie   I'm all right.

Ellen   I think I'll miss him. And I've not seen him for years. Just the thought, you know?

Charlie Yeah.

Ellen He was very good to me. He was a good boss.

Charlie Yeah.

Ellen Always gave me a lift home when it was raining.
Make us cups of tea. Muck in.

A slight pause.

Funny.

Charlie What?

Ellen Drinking in the afternoon.

A slight pause. She looks at him.

Would you mind if I went to the cinema tomorrow?

Charlie What's on?

Ellen I don't know. I was just going to show up. Go into
Manchester and just turn up. Buy a ticket. Go in. Wait and
see. (*Beat.*) I might walk.

Charlie Into Manchester?

Ellen Do you know, I've never done that. Not since I got
here.

Charlie It's 'cause it's fucking miles away.

Ellen I don't like it when you swear, you know. It sounds
odd.

A slight pause.

Have you ever done something, or thought something, or
acted in some way and known that afterwards your whole
life would never be the same again?

Charlie I don't know what you −

Ellen 'Cause I don't think I have for a long time.

Charlie Like what?

Ellen   I don't know. We should do something I think. Us two.

Charlie   What kind of thing were you thinking of?

Ellen   We could buy something. Do something unusual. Speak to Alice about the house. Sell up and go somewhere we've never been to before.

Charlie   Why?

Ellen   Just because we can.

Charlie   It starts off you want to go the cinema on yer todd and now you want to sell up and bugger off. I must admit I'm rather confused.

Ellen   I'm sorry. I'm just being a bit daft.

Charlie   A bit?

Ellen   You ever get a day like that?

Charlie   Like what, exactly? You've completely lost me.

A slight pause. She drinks.

Ellen   Peter should have come.

Charlie   I know.

Ellen   Did you not ask him?

Charlie   He was working.

Ellen   Or Alex. Or Christopher. It would have been appropriate. You'd have thought Alice would have brought them.

Charlie   He was my friend.

Ellen   I know.

Charlie   He was my friend. Not theirs.

Four

The deserted and derelict Bluebell Hotel, Edgely. **Christopher** *and* **Alex** *wait for* **Sarah**. *It is 8.30 on a Friday.*

Christopher   Get some more fags.

Alex   I'm waiting for Sarah.

Christopher   I'll wait for her.

Alex   She doesn't know you.

Christopher   I'll be dead nice to her.

Alex   She'll think you're weird.

Christopher   We'll run out.

Alex   Get yer own.

Christopher   They won't sell any to me. They think I look twelve.

Alex   'Cause yer do.

Christopher   Fuck off.

Alex   'Cause you are.

Christopher   It's half-eight. She should be here.

Alex   She will be.

Christopher   She better.

Alex   She will. Don't know why you wanted to meet here.

Christopher   'Cause it's fucking brilliant.

Alex   It's fucking freezing more like. We should have gone to the pub.

Christopher   If I can't buy fags they'll never let me in a pub.

Alex   Could have met her at home. Met her tomorrow.

Christopher   I wanted to meet her first. On neutral territory. You don't have to stay for long.

Alex   We won't. Don't worry.

Christopher   I can't believe Mum and Dad are letting her stay. Are you gonna have sex with her?

Alex   Fucking hell, Christopher.

Christopher   What?

Alex   What are you like? Your brain, Jesus!

Christopher *grins. Takes out a box of matches. Lights one. Holds it. Tries to burn it all black by holding both ends.*

Christopher   I should be at work.

Alex   What?

Christopher   I should. I'm down tonight. I rang in sick.

Alex   Fucking hell.

Christopher   They can't sack me. Can't sack somebody for being sick.

Alex   Everybody else'll be working late now.

Christopher   I wouldn't mind if they did, anyway. They're all weird.

Alex   It's just selfish.

Christopher   I think you're too good for that place, you know?

Alex   Honestly, Christopher.

Christopher   Breaking up boxes. You're quite clever when you put your mind to it.

Alex   Fucksake.

Christopher   And they're all retarded fuckheads who should be sterilised so that they don't breed and have retarded fuckhead babies I think.

Alex   Sarah works there.

Christopher   She might be a retarded fuckhead too for all
I know.

Alex   She isn't.

Christopher   I'm gonna quit.

Alex   Good.

Christopher   Sell drugs.

Alex   Good. Good.

Christopher   Rob houses.

Alex   Good.

Christopher   I'm serious, though. If you could be arsed
you could be right brainy. You could leave work. Leave
home. Leave Stockport. See the world. I reckon you'd be all
right. You lazy spas.

Sarah *enters.*

Sarah (*to* **Alex**)   Hello.

Alex   Hiya.

Sarah   Are you Christopher?

Christopher   Yeah. Hello.

Sarah   I'm Sarah.

Christopher   It's very nice to meet you, Sarah.

Sarah   It's very nice to meet you too. I love your hotel.

Christopher   Thank you.

Alex   You get in all right?

Sarah   I've never seen anywhere like it.

Christopher   Not many people know you can get in.

Alex   It's his fucking den.

Sarah   It's fantastic.

Christopher   I've heard a lot about you.

Sarah   Yeah. Me too.

Christopher   Alex says you're really lovely.

Sarah   He told me you were fucking crackers. (*Beat.*) Is it haunted here?

Alex   Don't be soft.

Sarah   It might be.

Christopher (*to* **Sarah**)   Do you believe in ghosts?

Sarah   I don't know. I've never seen one. But you can't tell, can you?

Christopher   I do. They completely terrify me. Have you got any fags?

Sarah   No. I can get some.

Christopher   We're running out.

Alex   You're a right scav.

Christopher   We are, though. Then you'll be sorry.

Sarah   Are we staying here for a bit?

Alex   I thought we could go to the pub.

Sarah   In a bit. Be good to explore.

Alex   There's not that much to explore, Sarah. Just empty rooms.

Sarah   Can we, please?

Christopher   Latent.

Sarah   What?

Christopher   The rooms, they're latent with potential.

Sarah   Right.

She looks at him as though he's insane and wanders off to explore.

Alex   Fucking hell.

Christopher   You can go if you want. The two of you.

Alex   She'll be here hours now. She's like that.

Christopher   She won't. She'll calm down after a bit.

Alex   I'm gonna go and get some fags. When I come back we'll fuck off.

Christopher   Good thinking.

Alex   Christopher.

Christopher   What?

Alex   Don't be fucking nutters, will yer?

Christopher   Don't be soft.

Alex   I mean it. I'll be a few minutes.

Christopher *watches him go. Makes sure he's gone and then gets out his box of matches and makes a 'genie'. He sticks three matches wedged out of the side of the box. Pulls out a fourth. Lights it. Lights the three sticking out and drops the box down. Watches the three matches burn down and the box burn into flames. As he does that* **Sarah** *comes back to watch him.*

Sarah   How long have you known about this place?

Christopher   About a year. Bit more.

Sarah   It's amazing, I think.

Christopher   I don't think it is haunted. I've never seen any ghosts here.

Sarah   When did it close down?

Christopher   Ages ago. My gran and grandad used to court here. When it was open. Obviously. I like the verb 'to court'.

Sarah   You'd've thought somebody would buy it.

Christopher   People are odd, I think.

Sarah   Is that your hobby?

Christopher   No.

Sarah   Where's Alex?

Christopher   He didn't say. He just walked off.

Sarah   Does that mean he's gone to get some fags.

Christopher   I don't know what it means. (*Pause.*) Googling.

Sarah   You what?

Christopher   Googling is my hobby. Looking things up on the Internet. It's mind blowing. Al Quaeda 48,700 hits in 0.16 seconds. The War On Terror 5,350 000 hits in 0.25 seconds. God. 56 900 000 hits in 0.55 seconds. Porn. 148 million hits in 0.20 seconds.

Sarah   How many did Roy Keane get?

Christopher   I've never tried him.

Sarah   Fucking loads, I bet.

Christopher (*turns to look at her*)   I hate football. It's really weird.

Sarah   Right.

Christopher   I'm very excited that you're going to be staying at our house.

Sarah   Are you?

Christopher   I'm quite surprised, though.

Sarah   Why?

Christopher   I think it's very enlightened of my parents.

Sarah   Enlightened?

Christopher   I thought they'd go completely insane. They still might.

Sarah I hope not.

Christopher You wanna watch them, though. They can be a little unpredictable.

Sarah Will they batter us?

Christopher No. They'll just give you funny looks. (*Beat. He's really staring at her.*) I'll get to see you in your 'jamas. That'll be quite funny. I'll make you both a cup of tea in bed in the morning.

Sarah Thanks.

Christopher Are you going to have sex with Alex, do you think?

Sarah You what?

Christopher I don't know if he's ever actually had sex before. He might not be very good at it. Don't judge him, will you?

Sarah Christopher, will you stop looking at me like that, please?

Christopher Sorry. (*He doesn't look away. Pause.*) Kiss me.

Sarah What?

Christopher Please.

Sarah Fucking hell.

Alex *comes back.*

Alex Fags.

No response.

Right.

He opens the packet. Lights one. Takes out ten more and puts them in an old packet. Throws the packet to **Christopher**.

Turns to **Sarah**.

Alex Should we go?

Five

Charlie *and* **Ellen***'s house. The living room.* **Charlie** *is showing* **Christopher** *a magic trick. It is 11 a.m. on Saturday.* **Charlie** *is drinking a glass of high-strength cider.*

Charlie   Pick a card.

Christopher *picks a card from the pack.*

Charlie   Don't show me what it is. Now. Put it back in the pack.

Christopher *does.*

Charlie   And shuffle.

He does.

More.

He does.

Now cut the pack.

He does.

And again.

He does.

And again.

He does.

Now give me the pack.

He does.

(*Taking a drink.*)   Watch this.

Charlie *taps the top of the pack hard three times and cuts the pack. Reveals the top card of the bottom half.*

Charlie   Is that your card?

Christopher   How the fuck did you do that?

Charlie   It's a good job I didn't bet you.

Christopher   No. How did you, though?

Charlie   I could've cleaned you out.

Christopher   I'm gobsmacked.

Charlie   You should be.

Christopher   Are they all the same card or something?

Charlie   No.

Christopher   Is it an optical illusion, Grandad?

Charlie   Is it a what?!

Christopher   I don't know what to say.

Charlie   Then say nowt. It's magic. Comes from years of experience.

Christopher   Is Gran in?

Charlie   I've not seen her.

Christopher   Where is she?

Charlie   I've no idea.

Christopher   Have you got any cigarettes you could give me?

Charlie (*looks at him*)   You what?

Christopher   Have you, Grandad?

Charlie   I don't smoke, Christopher. Not for years.

Christopher   Course you do.

Charlie   I don't, you know.

Christopher   I can always tell. It's written all over your face.

Beat.

Charlie   How old are you?

Christopher   Go on.

Charlie *shakes his head. Pulls a packet of cigarettes out of his pocket. Gives one to* **Christopher***, lights one himself.*

Charlie   Don't tell yer gran. She'd go crackers.

Christopher   Right. Don't tell my dad either. His head'd explode probably. You should open a window when I'm gone.

Charlie   I will.

Christopher   And get some Polos. I'd eat a whole packet if I were you.

Charlie *looks at him. The two smoke for a bit.* **Christopher** *watches him drink.*

Christopher   I'm sorry your friend died.

Charlie   Thank you.

Christopher   Was he incredibly old?

Charlie   No. He was just ill. He was my age.

Christopher   Is that frightening?

Charlie   Why frightening?

Christopher   That people your own age have started to die on you?

Charlie   I've not really thought about it.

Christopher   It would frighten me.

Charlie *(smiles at him)*   You staying for a cup of tea?

Christopher   I can't. I'm going shopping.

Charlie   Shopping?

Christopher   Yeah. Have you got some money you could lend me?

Charlie   You what?

Christopher   Or give me. I'm not sure I'll be able to pay it back.

Charlie   What you want money for?

Christopher   You know Alex has got a new girlfriend?

Charlie   I did hear something about that.

Christopher   She's staying round ours tonight. She's fucking amazing. I thought I'd buy her a present.

Charlie   Why do you want to do that?

Christopher   To welcome her to the house. They might get married or anything. You never know.

Charlie   Don't you think Alex is the one who should be buying her presents?

Christopher   That's why. Be more of a surprise coming from me. Be more delightful.

Charlie *looks at him for a bit. Puts his cigarette out.*

Charlie   How much do you need?

Christopher   A hundred pounds.

Charlie   Don't be ridiculous.

Christopher   A fiver, then.

Charlie   A fiver?

Christopher   I'll get her something cheap. Get something for my lunch and all.

Charlie   What you gonna get her?

Christopher   I'll get her a photograph of Roy Keane I think. She's very in love with Roy Keane.

Charlie   Right.

Christopher   I think he's fucking ugly. I think he's got a weirdly shaped face. But she's completely smitten.

Charlie   Right. Here.

He unpeels a fiver from his wallet and passes it over.

Christopher   Thanks, Grandad.

Charlie   That's all right. (*Drinks some cider.*) You sure you don't want a cup of tea?

Christopher   No. I don't want to miss the shops.

Charlie   It's only eleven o'clock.

Christopher   I know. Don't tell Gran, will you?

Charlie   Why not?

Christopher   I'd hate her to think I was getting in debt.

Charlie   Right.

Christopher   Or Mum. Or Dad. Or anybody.

Charlie   Righto.

Christopher   Debt's a terrible thing. It's completely paralysing.

Six

In **Peter** *and* **Alice**'*s house, in their kitchen,* **Sarah** *is waiting for* **Alex** *with* **Peter**. *It is 11.00 a.m. on Saturday.* **Peter** *is making them both a cup of tea.*

Sarah   He asked me to kiss him.

Peter   Did he?

Sarah   He kept looking at me.

Peter   Right.

Sarah   Is he a little bit mentally ill?

Peter   Is he what?

Sarah   It just struck me that he might be.

Peter   I don't think so, love, no.

Sarah   Maybe you should do some tests.

Peter (*handing her her tea*)   You wanna sit down?

Sarah   I'm all right.

He decides not to sit either.

Peter   He won't be long, probably. Lazy bugger.

Beat.

Sarah   Thank you for letting me stay tonight.

Peter (*drinks*)   That's all right.

Sarah   It's very kind of you. I'm quite excited as it goes. My house does my head in sometimes.

Peter   Why's that?

Sarah   Just people going on. It must be quite odd for you.

Peter   Odd?

Sarah   Is it the first time you've had one of Alex's girlfriends stay the night?

Peter   It is, yeah.

Sarah   Does it freak you out a bit?

Peter   No. Should it?

Sarah   I don't think so. But I think that if I had a kid, and I thought he was having sex, I think I'd find it a bit weird.

Peter   I don't. Just be careful.

A beat.

Sarah   I met Mrs Holmes the other week. I thought she was lovely.

Peter   She said. She said you were very smiley.

Sarah   Smiley?

Peter   That's what she said.

Sarah   God. People don't normally think that I'm smiley. People normally think I'm miserable.

Peter Alice didn't think so.

Sarah How long have you been married?

Peter Twenty years next July.

Sarah China.

Peter What?

Sarah Twenty years is your china wedding anniversary.

Peter I didn't know that.

Sarah I know all of them.

Peter Should I shout him again?

Sarah I don't believe in it, though.

Peter What?

Sarah That's one of the curious things about me. I know all of the wedding anniversary materials but I actually don't believe in marriage.

Peter Don't you?

Sarah I think it's repressive. I think it fucks people up. I think it stops people doing what they want to do. Shouldn't let it. Should just live, I think.

Peter It doesn't always.

Sarah What?

Peter Marriage, it doesn't always stop people from doing what they want to do.

Sarah You say that now.

Peter I mean it.

Sarah Have you been very loyal?

Peter I'm sorry?

Sarah Don't apologise. I was just wondering if you've been very loyal to your wife. If you've been completely monogamous.

Peter I don't think that's any of your business.

Sarah That means you haven't, doesn't it?

Peter No it doesn't. It means it's none of your business.
(*Beat.*) As a matter of fact, I have.

Sarah Have you?

Peter Yes.

Sarah I think that's wonderful.

Peter Yeah. I do too.

Sarah Hasn't it ever been a bit frustrating?

Peter What?

Sarah Being monogamous.

Peter I think I'm going to end this conversation.

Sarah I reckon you could be right filthy, you. Don't worry.
I think most men are. But I bet you could be, couldn't you?

No response.

Is it very strange, having two sons?

Peter In what way?

Sarah They're very different aren't they, Christopher and
Alex? I think they are. I really like both of them. I like Alex
because he's quite sensible. Do you like painting houses?

Peter Do I like it?

Sarah I imagine it's very satisfying, is it?

Peter I don't paint houses. I'm not a painter-decorator.
I restore buildings. It's different.

Sarah Right.

Peter I like working outside. Especially in the summer. But
in the winter too sometimes. I like getting a job finished and
leaving the house looking better than when you started it.

Sarah   Do you work with your top off in the summer?

Peter   I –

Sarah   Show us your muscles.

Peter   What?

Sarah   Go on. They're nice.

Long pause. He puts his tea down. He looks at her.

Peter   Do us a favour.

Sarah   What? (*Beat.*) What?

Peter   Don't fuck him about, Alex. Will you?

Sarah   No I won't. Course not.

Seven

Charlie *and* **Ellen***'s house. Their living room.* **Alice** *has called for* **Ellen***, who is out. It is Saturday morning. 11.30 am.*

Charlie   I leant him a fiver. He said he wanted to buy a present for Alex's girlfriend.

Alice   For Sarah?

Charlie   Is that what she's called?

Alice   What's he want to buy a present for Sarah for?

Charlie   I think he's a bit in love with her.

Alice   Right.

Charlie   He said she was staying over.

Alice   That's right.

Charlie   Tonight?

Alice   Yes, she is.

Charlie   I remember when you first came round. I thought you were lovely.

Alice   You didn't need to lend him any money.

Charlie   No. I wanted to. What's she like, Sarah?

Alice   I like her.

Charlie   You don't sound too sure.

Alice   She's lovely. No. I think she's very sweet.

Charlie   You're quite worried about her, aren't you?

Alice   No. Not in the least.

Charlie   I wouldn't. Boys are like that, aren't they? Peter was like that

Alice   I'm not in the least bit worried.

Charlie   You look it.

Alice   I'm not, Charlie. Can you tell Ellen I popped round to see if she needed – ?

Charlie   You want to open up a bit is what you want to do.

Alice   I want to what?

Charlie   Come on, Alice. You know what I'm talking about. You've got an eyelash.

He leans in to remove a stray eyelash before she can do it herself.

You've got good lips, you. You have. They're lovely. I always thought that.

Alice   I'm going to go now.

Charlie   I don't understand women sometimes. Ellen said to me yesterday, we got back from Angus's funeral, she started talking about selling up, about selling the house. She asked me to talk to you about it. Can you believe that?

Alice   –

He stares at her for a short time then smiles.

Charlie   I like Christopher. I think he's got an extraordinary mind.

Alice   Yes.

Charlie   But the amount of money he borrows off me, you wouldn't believe.

Alice   The amount of *money*?

Charlie   Are you sure you don't want a cup of tea?

Alice   No. Really. I have to go. How much money has Christopher been borrowing off you?

Charlie   It doesn't matter.

Alice   Charlie.

Charlie   It's not a problem. I promised him I wouldn't tell.

Eight

Outside **Susan Reynolds**' *house* **Peter Holmes** *is advising her about the restoration of the house's exterior supporting beams.* **Susan** *is in the very early stages of pregnancy. It doesn't really show at all yet. It is a bright February morning. The two of them shield their eyes from the sun as they look up at the wood.*

Peter   You have to be careful. You can get cracks.

Susan   Right.

Peter   If there's too much paint. Especially, see, where the wood is oldest. You have to be quite gentle.

Susan   Right.

He feels the wood of some lower beams. Tests it.

Peter   I can do it. It's not a problem.

Susan   Great.

Peter   But I'd be a bit reluctant to do it quickly.

Susan   Right.

Peter   Because that can just be damaging. I've seen people take a blow torch. Burn it all up. It's ridiculous. A gentle

chemical wash. Over time. Just take one or two layers off.
Are you in a terrible rush?

Susan Not, not, no, not massive.

Peter Because one thing might be to treat it over time.
Do one treatment a month. It wouldn't cost any more. And
because this is such an old house, and because the wood is
original and I don't want to damage it, then I might
recommend something like that.

Susan What would that involve?

Peter I could treat the whole house in about a day. Work
over the course of, say, a six-month period. And then the
wood would be properly prepared. It would really last. You
could apply a fresh colour and risk nothing from doing that.

Susan I'm actually pregnant.

Peter Right.

Susan So six months feels like a long time.

Peter I see. Well, that's just the safest way.

Susan I like the idea of it being safe.

Peter You can think about it. Get back to me.

Susan Right.

Peter I've got two of my own.

Susan Have you?

Peter Two boys.

Susan Boys are nice. How old are they?

Peter Alex is eighteen and Christopher's fifteen.

Susan Gosh. They're grown-ups.

Peter Yeah.

Susan I don't think I've ever been more excited about
anything.

Peter   It is a big thing.

Susan   Steven, my, my, my husband. He's started to worry. Worry about things.

Peter   You do.

Susan   The money and what it means in terms of us and whether we'll ever go out again.

Peter   It changes things.

Susan   Does it?

Peter   Lots of things.

Susan   I'm worried that I'm too old. I wanted, for work, to wait. I work in publishing. And there's always somebody who – There's this need to, to, to –

Peter   Push on.

Susan   Exactly. I'm sorry. I'm keeping you.

Peter   No, no. No, no.

Susan   On a Saturday as well.

Peter   That's not a problem. Maybe you need to have a think about what you want me to do.

Susan   Yes. No. I think. Can I ring you?

Peter   Of course you can.

Pause.

I don't see my two as much as I should. I go out with Christopher sometimes. We go for a bike ride every now and then. Or to the pub. I buy him a beer. That's all right. It's not the same as when they're very little.

Susan   He's too young to drink.

Peter   It doesn't matter.

Susan   Too many people drink, I think.

Nine

Charlie *and* **Ellen***'s house. Saturday afternoon. The living room.*
Ellen *is set to go to the cinema. Her coat is on. She busies around
the room collecting keys, glasses, bus-pass, tissues, money, etc.*
Charlie *stands dead centre of the room and watches her.*

Ellen   I can smell it. I'm not an idiot.

Charlie   Smell what?

Ellen   Lysterine. I'm going out now. I don't want to come
home and find you –

Charlie   Alice came round.

Ellen   Did she?

Charlie   She's a prying fucking cow, I think.

Ellen   What?

Charlie   Didn't want nothing. Comes round for no reason.
I told her, 'What do yer want?' She didn't know what to say.

Ellen   I don't know what time I'll be back.

Charlie   Told her to sling her hook.

Ellen   Right. Don't drink any more.

Charlie   Ha!

Ellen   I'll get a taxi. Don't, Charlie, I'm serious. (*Beat.*) And
don't wait up for me.

Charlie   You're not going.

Ellen   I don't think I'll be late but I don't want you
worrying.

Charlie   You're not going.

Ellen   Here.

She goes to kiss him goodbye.

He speaks before she reaches him.

Charlie   You're not going anywhere, Ellen, I told you.

Ellen Don't be silly.

Charlie I'm not being silly.

Ellen Charlie. I'll see you later.

Charlie I've not eaten.

Ellen You what?

Charlie I've not, Ellen, have I? I've not eaten.

Ellen Charlie, we talked about this, you said –

Charlie I've not eaten. What am I gonna do?

Ellen There's some money. Go to the chip shop.

Charlie I reckon I might go out. Go down Manchester meself. Go for a drink. Go dancing.

Ellen Charlie.

Charlie Gimme your keys.

Ellen Charlie.

Charlie Give them to me.

Ellen They're not your keys. They're mine. Charlie, for God's sake.

Charlie Give 'em.

Ellen No.

Charlie *grabs her by the arm, starts to push it behind her back.*

Charlie Gimme them. Now.

Ellen Get off.

Charlie Gimme them, Ellen.

Ellen You're hurting me.

Charlie I'll batter yer, Ellen. I swear. I'll –

Suddenly **Charlie** *pulls away from her as though punched in the stomach by complete surprise. Bends double over his knees. Begins to cough his lungs out.* **Ellen** *watches, largely unmoved.*

Christopher *has entered.*

Ellen You wouldn't. Would you? (*Beat.*) I'm tired of this, Charlie.

Christopher Gran? Are you all right?

Ellen Christopher? What are you doing here?

Christopher I came round to show Grandad the present I bought. What's going on?

Ellen Nothing, love. Nothing. Really.

Christopher Did he hit you?

Ellen No, love. Hit me? No. Course he didn't.

Christopher Is he all right?

Ellen He's fine, love, it's just his chest.

Christopher I don't believe this.

Ellen Seriously, Christopher, it's not what it looks like.

Christopher It's exactly what it looks like.

Ellen Don't be upset, love.

Christopher I'm not upset. I'm just a bit − I don't think I'll show him any more. I don't think he deserves it, do you?

Ten

Peter *and* **Alice**'s *house. The kitchen. The television is off.* **Alice** *is out.* **Peter** *and* **Christopher** *are alone. It is Saturday, after eight. They eat their way through a bowl of peanuts.* **Peter** *drinks a small bottle of beer.* **Christopher** *drinks a can of Coke. As they talk, eat and drink,* **Peter** *moves about, busying himself tidying the debris of the day in the house.*

Peter I've no idea.

Christopher Do you ever think about it?

Peter Sometimes.

Christopher   Do you think we'll still be around?

Peter   I think so, yes.

Christopher   Not blown ourselves up? Bombed ourselves to bits?

Peter   Not completely.

Christopher   Do you think we'll have jet packs?

Peter   Jet packs?

Christopher   To fly around in?

Peter   We might do.

Christopher   Hundred years *ago* there was nothing any good was there?

Peter   There were some things.

Christopher   Bicycles. Crap planes. That's about it. We've got loads of better stuff now. (*Pause.*) Can I tell you a secret?

Peter   Course.

Christopher   What time is it?

Peter   Half-eight.

Christopher   I read somewhere that the earth is going to be sucked into the sun in five thousand years time. That's not that long when you think about it, is it? (*Beat.*) That wasn't the secret, by the way.

Peter   Right.

Christopher   Do you think it's likely that there'll be a terrorist attack on Stockport ever?

Peter   I doubt it.

Christopher   I don't think we are living in transitional times, you know?

Peter   You what?

Christopher   One of our teachers said we were living in transitional times. The last three years. Nothing will ever be the same again. I think that's rubbish. Nothing's changed that much. Has it?

Peter   I don't know.

Christopher   Not really it hasn't. Still get Coke and that, can't you? Still go on bike rides. Go up the airport and watch the planes. Watch telly. Sit in yer garden. Smoke fags.

Peter   You don't smoke fags.

Christopher   How do you know?

Peter   I know. What's your secret?

Peter *stops tidying.*

Christopher *smiles. 'Lights' a pen/cigarette. Grins at his dad.*

Christopher   What time's Mum getting back?

Peter   She won't be long, I don't think.

Christopher   Is Sarah upstairs?

Peter   I think so.

Christopher   Have you met her?

Peter   Yeah. She came round earlier.

Christopher   What do you think they're up to?

Peter   I don't know.

Christopher   Can you hear them?

Peter   Christopher.

Christopher   I'm gonna get a glass and put it to the wall and listen in and see what they're doing.

Peter   You are not.

Christopher   I'm completely in love with her. That was my secret. I think she's absolutely amazing.

Peter   Right.

Christopher   I bought her a present. I bought her a beautiful photograph of Roy Keane. I bought it in a frame and everything. Got it for a fiver. I wanted to give it to her as soon as she got here but I missed my chance. I don't know what I'm going to do about it. I've been feeling sick in my stomach all day. But sick in a good way. I have been grinning and everything.

Peter   You've only met her the once, Christopher.

Christopher   I know. It is a bit mad.

Peter   She is very pretty.

Christopher   I know she is. It's more than that, though. Honestly. Do you think it's appalling?

Peter   Appalling? No. Not appalling.

Christopher   Can you take me out for a beer and talk about it?

Peter   If you want to.

Christopher   Do you think Alex would batter me if he found out?

Peter   I can't imagine Alex battering anybody really.

Christopher   I don't think he's good enough for her.

Peter   Chris –

Christopher   I'm completely serious about that, by the way. What do you think I should do about it?

Peter   Well. For now, I wouldn't necessarily worry about doing anything.

Christopher   I hardly slept last night for thinking about her.

Peter   It's a good thing, really, mate.

Christopher   Don't say that. You've obviously no idea what it's like.

Peter   I do, you know.

Christopher   Has it ever happened to you?

Peter   Has what?

Christopher   Falling completely in love with your brother's girlfriend? Has it?

Peter   I don't have a brother.

Christopher   Then how can you know what it's like? The idea that she's going to be asleep in the room next door to my bedroom drives me completely mental.

Eleven

Alex's *bedroom in* **Peter** *and* **Alice**'s *house.* **Alex** *and* **Sarah***.*

Sarah   I like your house.

Alex   Why?

Sarah   It's dead posh, I reckon.

Alex   Is it fuck posh.

Sarah   I think it is.

Alex   Well, it's not.

Sarah   I was chatting to your dad earlier. I think he fancies me.

Alex   Fuck off.

Sarah   I think it's true.

Alex   I don't blame him. I fancy you rotten.

Sarah   Clown.

Alex   I was gonna take you out but I didn't have any money.

Sarah   That's all right.

Alex   I was gonna go and buy you a meal or something. I will do. Soon.

Sarah   Right.

Alex   Borrow some money off our grandad. He'll lend us anything. He's all right. He's fucking loaded and all. He used to run Dad's company. Sold it to him. He's a bit tight, but I can get round him dead easily.

Sarah   You're funny.

Alex   Why?

Sarah   A meal?

Alex   What's wrong with that?

Sarah   Are you incredibly nervous?

Alex   No.

Sarah   You don't need to be.

Alex   I'm not.

Beat.

I love you.

She laughs.

Alex   Don't laugh.

Sarah   Sorry.

Alex   It's true. It feels like a dare.

Sarah   What?

Alex   To say it. But it is true, actually.

She kisses him.

Sarah   I got us some chocolates.

Alex   Did yer?

She produces a box of chocolates from her bag.

Sarah   Do you want a chocolate?

Alex   Yeah. All right. Thanks.

Sarah That's all right.

Alex Where d'yer get 'em?

Sarah Work. I nicked 'em.

Alex You never.

Sarah I did. Stupid mongs. Never notice anything.

They eat their chocolates. She puts a hand on her tummy.

Feel my tummy.

Alex What?

Sarah Here. Put your hand here. (*She moves his hand there.*)
Can you feel anything?

Alex Like what?

Sarah Sometimes I think I can feel a lump.

Alex I don't think you can normally feel stomach cancer
on the outside.

Sarah *reaches into her bag agin.*

She pulls out a contact lens case and a bottle of solution.

Turns back to **Alex***.*

Sarah Have you ever had sex before, Alex?

Alex What?

Sarah Have you?

Alex No.

Sarah Neither have I.

Alex Haven't you?

Sarah No.

She removes a contact lens and washes it as she speaks.

Everybody always thinks I have because of our sisters.
I haven't. It's not true.

Alex   Your sisters?

Sarah   Kirsty used to take boys to the cinema and wank them off for a fiver. And Lucy did it too for a bit. When I was in Year Seven they used to do that.

Alex   Right.

Sarah   I did it once. This lad asked me if I would. I think he thought it must have run in the family. It was fucking dead funny. He kept telling me I was doing it wrong. Couldn't get it up. And then did. And came on me. Should have seen his eyes. Like a dead person. It was just ridiculous. He gave us a tenner.

Alex   Great.

Sarah   (*turns back to him*)   But I've never had sex. Not properly. So you don't need to panic. Or be nervous.

Alex   I wasn't panicking.

Sarah   We don't even need to do anything.

Alex   You what?

Sarah   Tonight. We don't need to.

Alex   Don't you want to?

Sarah   Yeah. Course. But if you don't. We could maybe just sleep and that.

Alex   I don't think we could. I don't think I could.

Twelve

Peter *and* **Alice***'s kitchen. Sunday morning.* **Christopher** *is on his way out of the door.* **Peter** *has been frying bacon.* **Alice** *is in her dressing gown.* **Peter** *and* **Alice** *are drinking tea. A beautiful February morning.*

Peter   Have you eaten anything?

Christopher No.

Peter You've got to eat something, Christopher.

Christopher I'm not hungry. I'm going out.

Alice Where're you going?

Christopher I'm going for a ride. It's a beautiful day. Look at it. It's mad.

Alice Take an apple with you.

Christopher An apple?

Peter It is gorgeous, actually. We should go out somewhere.

Alice Put it in your bag. I'll make you a sandwich.

Christopher For breakfast?

Alex *and* **Sarah** *enter.*

Sarah Morning.

Alice Good morning.

Peter Morning, Sarah.

Sarah Hello.

Christopher Morning, Sarah.

Sarah Hello, Christopher.

Alex Mum, have you got any money I could borrow?

Alice Morning, Alex. How are you, Mum? I'm fine thank you, darling, how are you? I'm great, thanks.

Alex Morning, Mum.

Alice Morning. Are you two having breakfast?

Sarah I don't know. Maybe.

Peter I was gonna put some more bacon on.

Sarah That'd be smashing I think.

Alex (*drinking his mum's tea*) We're going out.

Sarah Are we?

Alex Sorry, Dad. We've not got time.

Christopher I wouldn't lend him any money if I were you, Mum, he'll spend it on drugs.

Alex Shut up.

Christopher It's true, isn't it, Sarah?

Sarah How are you this morning, Christopher?

Christopher I'm fine, thank you. How are you?

Sarah I'm great.

Christopher Did you sleep all right?

Sarah I did, thank you. Yes. It was lovely.

Christopher You look as though you slept well.

Peter You sure you don't want any bacon? I was cooking some anyway.

Christopher Doesn't she? Alex?

Alex No thanks, Dad, we're gonna be late.

Peter Where you off to?

Alex We're going to Manchester.

Peter On a Sunday?

Alex Going meeting some mates.

Christopher I think she does. I think you do.

Sarah Thank you.

Alice How much do you need?

Alex A tenner. I'll pay you back on Friday.

Alice (*passing him twenty pounds from her purse*) You will and all.

Alex   Thanks, Mum.

Peter *passes* **Alex** *a bacon sandwich that he's wrapped up in greaseproof paper.*

Peter   Here. Look. Take this with you.

Alex   What?

Peter   This one's made already. Take it with you.

Alex   I'm not hungry.

Sarah   I am. Thank you, Mr Holmes.

Peter   That's all right, Sarah. That's my pleasure.

Alice   You getting the bus?

Alex   Yep.

Alice   You coming home for tea?

Alex   Yep. I'll ring you.

Alice   Do you want to come round for your tea, Sarah?

Sarah   I don't think I can, Mrs Holmes.

Alice   Will you do me a favour? Will you call me Alice, love, please?

Sarah   Sorry. Yeah. I'm having tea at home tonight.

Alice   Right. That's okay. Well. You should. One time. It'd be lovely to see you.

Sarah   Thank you. That's really nice of you.

Alice   It was lovely to meet you.

Sarah   Yeah. Thanks for letting me stay.

Alice   That's all right.

Sarah   Thank you too, Mr Holmes.

Peter   Peter. Call me Peter. It's fine.

Alex   Yeah. Thanks, Mum. For. You know. We'll see you later.

Alice   Okay.

Alex   See you later, Dad.

Peter   See you.

Alex   See you later, bog-breath.

Christopher   See you later monghead.

Sarah   Bye, Alice. Peter.

Peter   Bye, love.

Alice   Bye-bye. I hope we'll see you soon.

Sarah   Yeah. I hope so too. Bye, Christopher.

Christopher   Bye.

Sarah   See you later.

Christopher   Yeah.

They watch them go. There's a long pause.

Alice   I'm gonna get dressed.

Peter   Right.

Alice   We should have a Sunday lunch one time. Ask her round.

Peter   We could do.

Alice   Maybe get Charlie and Ellen.

Peter   If you want.

Alice   I think she's all right.

Peter   I think so too.

Alice   Hmmm.

She leaves to get dressed.

Christopher   Could you hear them?

Peter   What?

Christopher   Last night. Alex and Sarah. Could you hear them?

Peter   Chris. Bloody hell.

Christopher   I couldn't hear anything. I tried using a glass. It didn't work.

Peter   Did you give her her present?

Christopher   No. I didn't. Too late now, I reckon.

Peter   Might not be.

Christopher   Is. I hate Roy Keane and all.

Peter   Where you going to?

Christopher   I'm gonna go up Ringway. Watch the planes.

Peter   You should take some lunch, you know?

Christopher   I'll be all right.

Peter   Here. Take one of these. They're all right cold. I like them.

He wraps a sandwich for him and gives it to him to put in his bag.

Christopher   Thanks.

Peter   Take an apple and all.

Christopher   Thanks, Dad.

Peter   There's some crisps in the cupboard. Take some crisps.

Christopher   Fucking hell.

Peter   Christopher!

Christopher   I'll burst, I'm telling yer.

Peter   You've got to eat.

Christopher   You're mad, you, I think.

Peter   I'll see you later.

Christopher   What you doing today?

Peter   I'm not sure. I might go to The Pineapple. Watch United.

Christopher   Who they playing?

Peter   Spurs. We should tank 'em.

Christopher   You could come with us.

Peter   You what?

Christopher   Could do. Could come with us to the airport. Come and watch the planes with us.

Peter   Maybe.

Christopher   You don't want to, do you?

Peter   It's not that.

Christopher   United are rubbish.

Peter   No they're not.

Christopher   Football's weird. You just want to go to the pub. It's bad for you. You should come out and get some exercise.

Peter   I know. I will. One time. Another day. I promise.

Christopher   Yeah.

Peter   I do. I promise you.

Christopher   All right.

Peter   Chris, don't worry about it. Sarah and that.

Christopher   Yeah.

Peter   He'll get bored with her. She'll dump him. She's probably completely mad.

Christopher   Yeah.

Peter   You're not the first person who it's ever happened to, you know?

Christopher   No. I know.

Peter   It happens all the time. It's people. It's what we're like.

Christopher   Yeah.

Peter   Don't be late, will you?

Christopher   No, no. No. No. I'll ring you if I will be.

Christopher *exits.*

Peter *watches him leave.*

Part Two

Alex

One

May 2004. The Bluebell Hotel. **Alex** *and* **Sarah** *are there with* **Alex**'s *friend* **Paul Danziger**. **Paul** *is wearing a long-sleeved Man United shirt with 'No. 6 STAM' on the back.*

Paul   Alex said you've never been to London before.

Sarah   I haven't, no.

Paul   If you came down I could take you out. Show you round. Be your tour guide. Where do you wanna go?

Sarah   I don't know.

Paul   Houses of Parliament. Buckingham Palace. Westminster Abbey. Tower of London. London Eye. London Dungeons. London Bridge. Hyde Park Corner. Trocadero. Piccadilly Circus. Leicester fucking Square. We can do all that. No bother.

Sarah   Thanks.

Paul   Do you want some of this?

He offers them a rolled-up cigarette.

Sarah   No thank you.

Alex   What is it?

Paul   Its Solpadeine.

Alex   Right.

Paul   Which is a codeine-based painkiller. I like it. Does wonders for your agitation levels. Here y'are. Try it.

Alex   Thanks.

Alex *takes some. Smokes it.*

Paul It takes a bit of time. Gets there in the end. Marvellous stuff.

He watches **Alex** *smoke. Turns to* **Sarah**.

Do you like my shirt?

Sarah What?

Paul My shirt, do you like my shirt?

Sarah I do, yeah, it's –

Paul Very fucking rare these, you know? Long sleeves. Makes them exceptional. An unusual commodity. I got it on Ebay. Honest. I saved up. Ebay's extraordinary. Get anything. Are you a red?

Sarah I am, yeah.

Paul Nice one.

Sarah I like Roy Keane best.

Paul Is that right?

Sarah It is, yeah.

Paul Fair enough. Fair play to yer, girl. I think he's a fucking bender myself. I think he's a shirt-lifter, if I'm being honest with you. I think he's a bit of an arse-bandit. Bit of an old uphill gardener. Bit of a chocolate fudge-packer, you with me?

Sarah He's better than Jaap Stam.

Paul Yer reckon?

Sarah Jaap Stam doesn't even play for United any more. Plays for AC Milan.

Paul See, that doesn't really matter to me. I've got a very refined sense of loyalty I think. (*About the Solpadeine.*) How do you like it?

Alex It's good. Yeah. It's great.

Sarah I won't be long. Stay here.

She leaves to explore the hotel again.

They watch her go.

Alex *pulls out a box of matches. Lights one and lets it burn.*

Turning it in his fingers so that the whole match is burnt to black.

Paul   When you get down, Alex, if you want anything, you want me to sort you out with anything – pills, grass, speed, charlie, smack, crack, uppers, downers, anything at all mate – you just ask me, I'll see you all right. I know loads of folk down there.

Alex   Nice one.

Paul   It's fucking lovely to see you again.

Alex   Yeah. You too mate.

Paul   How long's it been now?

Alex   Fucking two years.

Paul   Is it as long as that?

Alex   I think it is, yeah.

Paul   Fucking. Look at you. You're all skinny. Aren't you? You get any thinner you'll blow away.

Alex   You sure it's all right to crash at yours?

Paul   Course. I've got loads of room. It'll be fucking smart.

Alex   I don't think it'll be for very long. We want to try and find a place of our own.

Paul   You stay as long as you need to, mate. What's mine is yours. You're very welcome to all of it.

Alex   Nice one.

Paul   Remember when I stayed at yours?

Alex   Yeah.

Paul   That was fucking funny, wasn't it?

Alex Yeah.

Paul I thought it was a right laugh.

Alex Yeah.

Paul And your mum and everything. What was she like?
I used to quite fancy her, as it goes. Did I ever tell you that?

Alex No.

Paul I did and all. I was on your sofa. She'd come in,
in her nightie. See us in me sleeping bag. It was quite
embarrassing for me sometimes. She was lovely to me and
all. She was very kind. They both were, your mum and your
dad.

Alex They really liked you.

Paul How are they? Your mam and dad and that? They
all right are they?

Alex Yeah.

Paul They all right about you coming down?

Alex Yeah. They're not bad. You know. They're –

Paul Six billion people in this world.

Alex What?

Paul Six billion. One don't mean so much. Out of six
billion. When you think of it like that. Does it?

Alex I don't know.

Paul It doesn't. It doesn't mean so much.

Pause.

He lights another match.

Not been in this place for years. You remember when it was
open?

Alex No.

Paul *keeps the flame burning or lights a new match.*

Stares at **Alex** *while he talks, clocking his reaction.*

Alex *doesn't move.*

Paul *grins as he speaks.*

Paul   All t' fucking wood in here! Imagine this place and it's on fire! Be fucking . . .

Sarah *comes back.*

Paul *watches her re-enter.*

Shakes his match out.

Beat.

Paul   It's a bit mental being back, you know?

Alex   How's it mental?

Paul   It's like going back in time. All them folk. Still here with their little jobs and their little houses and their little mortgages and their little children and all that. Makes my head feel like it's bursting.

Alex   Right.

Paul   London's miles better.

Sarah   Why?

Paul   Better shops. Better houses. Better streets. Better people. People don't fucking talk to you all the time. People don't want to look at you and get under your skin and do all that. And sometimes you need a bit of space and everything, don't you? Need to get away from it all. I imagine that's exactly how you're feeling now, Alex, eh? Fucking all this.

Alex   Sometimes it is yeah.

Paul   I've hardly seen my folks since I've been back. Spent more time on me tod.

Sarah   Why's that, Paul?

Paul   You what?

Sarah   Why haven't you been to see your folks?

Paul   Just 'cause, just 'cause, just 'cause. Fucking. They're a bit – You know?

Beat.

Sarah   Yeah.

Paul (*to* **Alex**)   But I miss you, mate.

Alex   Do you?

Paul   Out of everybody. You're the one who's most all right.

Alex   Thanks.

Alex *passes him back the cigarette. He takes a big suck on it.*

Paul   So three months, you two?

Alex   Yeah.

Paul   Be married next. Pair of you. I'll be your best man. Make a speech and everything. I'd love that. It's really nice to meet you, Sarah.

Sarah   It's nice to meet you, too.

Paul   He's always going on about you, you know? When you're out of the room his little face drops and everything.

Alex   Paul!

Paul   Well, it's true. (*He stares at* **Sarah** *for a short time.*) God!

Sarah   What?

Paul   Your eyes!

Sarah   What about them?

Paul   They're like pools.

Sarah   Right.

He looks away again.

He finishes the cigarette. Puts it out.

Paul   Don't bottle it, will you?

Alex   What?

Paul   You. Coming down. Don't chicken out, mate. You know what I mean?

Two

Alex *and* **Sarah** *in* **Alex**'s *bedroom. Two days later. 1.30 a.m. on a Friday morning. There is a long time before either one of them speaks.* **Sarah** *wears glasses.*

Alex   You packed yet?

Sarah   Nearly. Not quite. I don't know what I'm gonna take.

Alex   Don't take too much. Don't pack like a girl.

Sarah   Fuck off.

A pause.

Is Paul gonna pick us up, do you know?

Alex   I don't think so. We'll just get a taxi.

A slight pause.

Alex   It's our anniversary. Three months tonight. Since you first stayed. Did you know that?

Sarah   No.

Alex   I keep track.

Slight pause.

I love making you come. It's like you're having an electric shock.

She smiles. Moves into him slightly.

He lights two cigarettes with one match and passes one to her.

Alex What did work say?

Sarah Nothing really. I was a bit disappointed. They just wanted to know when so they could get somebody in.

Alex Did you tell them you were going with me?

Sarah Course. Didn't you?

Alex I didn't think it was any of their business. (*Beat.*) Have you told your folks yet?

Sarah Not yet.

Alex What do you think they'll say?

Sarah I don't think they'll be bothered. I don't think they'll say anything.

Alex They probably will, you know.

Sarah You don't know them.

A slight pause.

Alex I've not told mine either.

Sarah You what?

Alex I haven't.

Sarah Fucking hell, Alex.

Alex I had to hide the tickets from them. I thought they'd go mad.

Sarah Alex, you've got to tell them.

Alex I will.

Sarah Jesus.

Alex What?

Sarah I think they might get a bit upset.

Alex I know.

Sarah I think they will.

Alex I know, all right?

Pause.

Sarah Is your dad working tomorrow?

Alex I don't know. I don't think so. He doesn't really go to work at the moment. Grandad's been working for him.

Sarah Well then, tell them tomorrow.

Alex Fucking hell, Sarah.

Sarah Alex, it's serious. What are you gonna do, just leave? Cheerio, Mum, just out for a packet of chips. See you in a few years.

Alex No!

Sarah Well, what's the use in putting it off? Who does that help?

Alex I'm not putting off. I'm just choosing the right moment.

Sarah Which is when?

Alex I don't know.

Sarah There's no right moment, Alex. The right moment is as soon as you can possibly do it, Alex. It's tomorrow. It's as soon as you wake up.

Pause. She takes out her vial of pills and takes one.

I'm gonna stop taking these, I think. I don't think I need them any more. I don't even feel sad.

Beat.

Alex Can I ask you something?

Sarah Course.

Alex Before we go. I was thinking. Can we go up to the Bluebell? Sleep out? Spend the night there?

Sarah Fucking hell.

Alex What?

Pause.

Sarah Are you having second thoughts?

Alex Don't be soft.

Sarah I'm not being soft. You might be. You might've changed your mind. I wouldn't blame you.

Alex I haven't.

Sarah Are you sure?

Alex I'm dead sure.

Sarah Well then. (*Beat.*) Tomorrow.

Three

The next morning. **Peter** *and* **Alice***'s kitchen.* **Alex** *has made his mum a cup of tea. She is in her dressing gown.*

Alex I made you some tea. Here.

Alice Thanks.

Alex You all right?

Alice I'm fine, love, yeah.

Alex You sure?

Alice I thought I heard something.

Alex What?

Alice I think it was probably just the roof. The roof creaks in the wind. I've noticed that.

Alex It's always done that. Where's Dad?

Alice He's out. He's gone to work.

Alex I thought Grandad was working for him

Alice There was another job came in. He didn't want to go.

Alex Right.

Pause.

There's something I have to tell you.

A long pause. She puts her tea down and studies his face for a sign.

Alice I'm not sure I want to hear this, do I?

Alex I don't know. (*Pause.*) Me and Sarah, we're thinking of going away.

Alice Away?

Alex We're thinking of going to stay with Paul Danziger for a bit.

A slight pause.

Of going down to London and trying to live in London for a bit.

A slight pause.

I don't know how long for. But for more than just a holiday.

Pause.

Just to see what it's like. Neither of us have ever lived anywhere else but round here. And we wanted to. And I know it's about the worst possible . . . the worst time that I could possibly choose, but there's nothing I can do about that.

Alice Right.

Alice *starts to nod her head.*

Alex I don't know if I can bear it at the moment. Round here. I feel sick all of the time.

Alice Right.

Alex I think if I stayed then I'd go mad. And Sarah wants to come with me.

Alice I see.

Alex Mum, I'm really sorry.

A very long pause.

Alice   I don't know what to say.

Pause.

Have you told your dad yet?

Alex   No.

Alice   But this is all decided. You've made all the plans. Everything's arranged. Paul knows. He's expecting you.

Alex   Yeah.

Alice   You'll have to tell them at work.

Alex   I already did.

Alice   You what?

Alex   I already did. I already told them.

Alice   You told them before you told me.

Alex   I –

Alice   Why? (*Beat.*) Why did you tell work before you told me?

Alex   Don't, Mum.

Alice   Jesus, Alex! Were you scared of me?

Alex   Not *of* you. I was scared of telling you. That's different.

Pause.

Alice   When are you thinking of going?

Alex   We've got the tickets.

Alice   You?

Alex   We have. We got them.

Alice   When for? (*Beat.*) Alex?

Alex   For Monday.

Alice (*laughs out loud*)   For what?!

Alex   For Monday, Mum.

Alice (*still laughing*)   Are you serious?

Alex   I'm sorry.

Alice (*still laughing*)   You're sorry?! My God, Alex, have you any idea what you're saying to me?

Alex   I –

Alice   Well, you can't, Alex. You can't go.

He can't look at her. He says nothing for a while.

Alex   I'm –

Alice   It's completely absurd. We haven't talked about this. You just decided! How long have you been thinking about this for, Alex? Well?

Alex   For a while now.

She picks up her tea and takes a huge, thirsty slug from it.

Alice   For a *while*? A *while*! Well then. That makes all the difference.

Alex   Mum.

Alice   No, Alex, Mum nothing. This is . . . You selfish, selfish little boy.

She turns away from him. She drops her teacup. It breaks and spills the tea. She ignores it.

He goes over to her and tries to touch her but can't.

She gives a big exhalation of breath and looks back to him.

I think I'd like to go and live somewhere else. Too. But not London. God! I'd go on my own. Go and live somewhere in the sun. Go to Spain. Pick oranges. What would you say if I did that?

Alex   I don't know.

Alice   What would you think?

Alex   It's your life.

Alice   I wish it had been him who'd – You know? Your dad. I think about that nearly all the time.

Four

Susan Reynolds' *house. Susan Reynolds is talking to* **Peter Holmes**, *who is dressed in overalls. He lays out a tray of chemical washes and a series of small brushes. He arranges his tray with a great deal of care and precision as he talks to her. When his tray is ready he begins to prepare a chemical mix. Pouring two chemicals into one bottle. Stirring them. Getting the measures as exact as he can.*

Susan   We don't know the date exactly. It was the parsonage. For St Paul's.

Peter   Yeah, you can tell that.

Susan   But we think it's a lot older than any of the other buildings round here.

Peter (*looking up from his work*)   I'm sure it is. By a bit, I'd say.

Susan   You see photographs of the road and there's no other buildings but the church and this house. There are fields. And then the church and then the house. And that's it.

Peter   I like old photographs.

Susan   Yes.

Peter   The people always dress quite oddly.

Susan   They don't look like real people, I think. I think they look more like cartoons.

Peter (*smiles*)   I should crack on.

He resumes work.

Susan   Right. Yes. Of course.

She watches him work for a short while.

Would you like a cup of tea?

Peter   I'm all right, actually.

Susan   If you wanted to put the radio on I could get you a radio.

Peter   No. I'm fine, honestly.

Susan   Right. I'll leave you to it. I'll just be upstairs.

He turns to her, pauses in his work.

Peter   How've you been getting on with my dad?

Susan   Fine. He's lovely. I like him. He's very charming. Where is he today?

Peter   He's doing another job. Out in Buxton. I'm sorry that I've not been around more. It's been quite a strange time.

Susan   He must be very proud of you, I think. How long have you been running the –

Peter   Six years.

Susan   It's such unusual work. You do a lovely job of it.

Peter   Thank you.

Susan   But he still works with you occasionally.

Peter   Not that often. Just recently.

Susan   Why's that?

Peter   Sorry?

Susan   Why's he started working with you more?

A pause.

He looks at her.

He resumes work before he talks.

Peter   To be honest, I've been a bit poorly.

Susan   Oh. Oh. Oh I'm sorry to hear that. I hope it's nothing, it's not serious, is it?

Peter   No. No. No. I've – There was an accident, actually.

Susan   An accident?

He stops work.

Looks at her.

Peter   My boy, Christopher, my youngest. He was out on his bike. On the – Just by the – going down the A6. There was. He was hit by a car. He was killed.

Susan   Oh my God.

Peter   Yeah.

Pause. He continues to work for a bit, then looks at her for a bit, then continues to work again.

It was nobody's fault. Well. It. I don't think he was riding too well. He shouldn't have been out riding where he was. I think he turned on some red lights. He didn't think. It wasn't the driver's fault or anything like that. It was an accident. (*Beat.*) I was the only one in the house as it goes. I got to the hospital before he . . . (*Turns to her.*) You know?

Susan   Oh, I'm so sorry.

Peter   Thank you. (*Works again.*) So I thought, I just needed a – a bit of time off. (*Turns to her.*) Sorry, you don't need to know this.

Susan   No no no no. It's fine. Really.

Peter   You blame yourself a bit, don't you? You try not to. But. You can't help thinking there are things you could've done. If I'd – you know.

Susan   When was this?

Peter   It was a few months ago. It's been very difficult. For Alice, my wife, as well, you know. And Alex, the eldest, it's difficult because he doesn't seem to be at all bothered by it. But – (*Pause.*) Sorry. I'm really sorry. I should crack on.

Long pause.

Sorry, I shouldn't have told you.

Susan   No. No. No. No. I'm sorry. That's just awful. I'm really – I'm glad you did.

Peter   We just need to see how things are going. Next month it might be my dad comes back. I want to take my wife abroad for a bit. Maybe go to, I don't know, go to, go to, go to, go somewhere.

Susan   You should do.

Peter   We'll see.

Susan   Somewhere hot.

Peter   Yes.

Susan   I don't know what to say to you.

Peter   No, I know. I'm sorry.

Susan   No. Don't be. Don't. You're sorry! I'm – I mean. God!

Peter   I should get cracking.

Susan   Please, Peter. You shouldn't worry about coming back to work or anything until you're absolutely ready to.

He looks right at her.

Peter   Thank you. I can't, sometimes – I can't get it out of my head.

Five

Peter *and* **Alex** *and* **Sarah** *on a footbridge overlooking the motorway. Watching the cars.* **Alex** *and* **Sarah** *are smoking.*

Alex   I like it here. It's fucking mental.

Peter *laughs.*

Sarah *watches him.*

Peter   I like in when there's a traffic jam. (*Pause.*) See everybody in their cars with their sandwiches. Or listening to music, singing along to it, maybe. Tapping their fingers. Nodding their heads.

Picking out a car.

Look at him.

Alex   Where?

Peter   Blue Renault.

Alex   Oh yeah!

Peter   Bet he does a guitar solo.

They watch for a bit then burst out laughing.

Alex   Dickhead.

Pause.

Peter   What'll you do for money?

Alex   I'll get a job. Both of us will.

Peter   Doing what?

Alex   I don't know yet. But doing something. Could get a reference from work easily. Maybe even get a job in a different branch. Sainsbury's all over London.

Peter   What rent's Paul gonna charge you?

Alex   He didn't say. Nothing for a bit. We'll give him something.

Peter   It's an expensive place, you know.

Alex (*pulls out a packet of cigarettes*)   I know.

Peter   Rent's expensive. Travel's expensive. Food's expensive. All of it is.

Alex *takes two cigarettes out of the packet. Lights them both.*

Alex   Get paid more, though.

Peter   Not much more, Alex.

Alex *gives* **Sarah** *a lit cigarette.*

Sarah   Thanks.

Peter   How's he keeping, Paul?

Alex   He's all right, I think.

Peter   Is he?

Alex   I think so.

Peter   What kind of place has he got?

Alex   He's got a flat. Got a spare room and all.

Peter   What about your mates?

Alex   I'll stay in touch with the ones who matter. That won't be a problem. They can come down and visit.

Peter   You won't know anybody.

Alex   I'll know Paul. He'll have mates.

Peter   Yeah.

Beat.

Monday?

Alex   Yeah.

Peter   Well, I'll give you something, Alex, your timing's cracking. Very sensitive. I can't wait to hear what your mother has to say about this.

Alex   I'm sorry.

Peter   What time's your train?

Alex   Half-eleven. Just after.

Peter   Can you get it from Stockport?

Alex   You can. Yeah.

Peter   Why didn't you talk to us, Alex?

Alex   It's not been very easy to talk to anyone about anything round here for ages.

Peter   Well, you could have tried, mate. Could've talked to me. I would've liked to have known. Fucksake.

Alex   Dad, don't.

Pause.

Peter   If I asked you not to go that wouldn't change anything would it? If I just turned round and asked you to wait or to think about it or to not go at all. It wouldn't though, would it?

Alex   I . . . No. No, it wouldn't, Dad. Not now. No.

Six

Peter *and* **Alice***'s kitchen.* **Peter** *and* **Alice**.

Alice   What did you say?

Peter   I didn't really know what to say.

Alice   That doesn't surprise me.

Peter   Don't.

Alice   Well, it doesn't, Peter. I can just see you. Him telling you and you just standing there. (*Imitating, a horrible mocking voice.*) 'Right. Right. Right. Right.' I mean, look at you!

Peter   Nothing I could have said would have made any –

Alice   I look at you like that and I don't blame him really.

Peter   Alice.

Alice   Has he packed?

Peter   I don't know.

Alice   I should help him. His train's just after half-eleven. Will you take them to the station or do you want me to?

Peter   No, I will.

Alice   Because I can. If you can't be bothered. Maybe there's something on the telly you want to watch. Or you might need to read the paper. Or listen to the fucking radio or something.

Peter   I'll do it. I'll do it. I said. Alice. Fucking hell!

Alice   What? (*No response.*) What, Peter?

Peter   I told you I'll take him.

Alice   If you wake up in time.

Peter   Will you please just be quiet! Just for one second!

Seven

Alex's bedroom. Night. **Alex** *and* **Sarah** *stand by the bed. She daren't touch him at first.*

Sarah   That was all right. Wasn't it?

No response.

You all right?

Alex   No.

Sarah   You're shaking.

Alex   Shut up.

Sarah   Come here.

He goes over to her. Starts sobbing. She holds him.

Alex Fucking hell.

Sarah Ssshhhh. Hey. Hey. Come on.

Alex Don't. It'll only make it worse.

Sarah He was all right, wasn't he?

Alex Not really. Not for him.

Sarah I thought he was quite good about it.

Alex You don't know him.

Sarah He's just a bit concerned.

Alex He's completely fucking –

Sarah What?

Alex Nothing. Don't matter.

She strokes the back of his head.

Sarah Was it horrible telling your mum?

No response.

I wish you'd let me come with you.

No response.

I wouldn't have minded.

Alex She broke a cup.

Sarah You what?

Alex Mum. She dropped her teacup. Hot tea in it and everything. Splashed her. She didn't even notice. Fucking hell, Sarah.

She holds him tighter.

Sarah Hey. Hey. Hey. Come on.

Holds him for a while.

You can stay, you know? If you think it would make it easier.

Alex No.

Sarah You can do. Come down in a bit, maybe.

Alex It wouldn't make any difference.

Sarah I could always go down first. Find us somewhere.

Alex Don't be stupid.

Sarah I could do it, though. If it'd make you happier.

Alex Sarah.

Sarah I wouldn't mind.

Alex (*smiles*) Liar.

Sarah I'm not lying.

Alex You fucking are.

Pause.

Sarah (*smiling slightly*) Well. Maybe a little, I am.

The two of them start chuckling slightly.

Alex Don't laugh. It's not funny.

Sarah (*laughing more openly*) I'm not laughing.

Eight

Charlie *and* **Ellen***'s living room.* **Charlie** *and* **Ellen**. *Later that night.* **Ellen** *is drinking a cup of tea.*

Charlie I don't mind, you know. You can go out whenever you want. You don't need to ask my permission.

Ellen You've said that before.

Charlie Get dolled up. Put your frock on. That doesn't bother me. I like it. I like to look at you.

Ellen Good.

Charlie You used to do that, didn't you?

Ellen Yes.

Charlie Why don't you ever do that any more?

Ellen Do what?

Charlie Wear something.

Ellen I don't know.

Charlie Come here. Let me look at you.

Ellen You can see me from there.

Charlie Come here Ellen. Come on. I want to see you up close.

Ellen Charlie.

Charlie Come on, love.

She moves one or two steps closer.

Ellen There. You can see me now.

Charlie Come here.

Ellen Charlie.

Charlie Come on.

He moves right up close to her. Starts unbuttoning her blouse.

Ellen Charlie, don't.

Charlie Here. Just a button. Is all. Looks good.

Ellen I'm − Don't.

Charlie You're still. I still find you attractive, Ellen. You know.

Ellen I know.

Charlie And it's all about − I want this washing machine. I want this Hoover. When was the last time you wore clothes for me?

Ellen What?

Charlie   When was it? When was it, love?

Ellen   I wear clothes for you all the time.

Charlie   You don't.

Ellen   I do, Charlie.

Charlie   I should know. Shouldn't I?

Very long pause. **Charlie** *holds on to the buttons of her blouse.*
Ellen *daren't move.*

I mean, look at you, Ellen.

A slight pause.

Your fault, this.

Ellen   Don't.

Charlie   My temper. Everything. It's not me, it's you.

Beat.

You should've stayed in fucking Nottingham.

Then **Charlie** *smiles and lets her go. He drinks. Coughs hard into
his hand. Looks to see what he's coughed up. Moves away from her.
Pulls out a cigarette from his pocket. Lights it. Smokes.*

Ellen   What are you doing?

Charlie   I'm smoking a cigarette.

He grins at her.

Nine

Alice *and* **Peter***'s kitchen.* **Alice** *is with* **Ellen***. Sunday afternoon.*
Alice *is in her dressing gown.*

Ellen   Alice, Charlie's not well.

Alice   –

Ellen It's his chest. He's been, he went to the doctor's. I wanted to come and tell you myself.

Alice Christ.

Ellen I didn't want to tell you on the phone. Or you to find out from anybody else.

Alice Is it serious?

Ellen They don't know yet.

Alice Ellen, I'm sorry.

Ellen He didn't want to tell you. He didn't want you to worry.

Alice Don't be silly. Of course we'd want to know. I'll tell Peter.

Ellen Yes. Do. How are you, love?

Alice I'm fine.

Ellen Are you?

Alice Yes. I'm good. I'm getting – You know? I've been thinking about going back to work.

Ellen Have you?

Alice I think I need to get out of the house.

Ellen You do.

Alice Just to get out and do something.

Ellen Sometimes we have to, don't we?

Alice I think so.

Ellen Sometimes, when there's something awful. We need to shake off the weight of things. Get them and give them a good shake.

Alice That's what I'm talking about.

Ellen Because it's not fair, is it? To stew.

Alice   I don't think so.

Ellen   I wanted to tell you that.

Alice   What?

Ellen   I think that you've been stewing a bit, haven't you?

Alice   Ellen?

Ellen   And I don't think it's fair to Peter. Or to Alex, actually. That might be one of the reasons why he's leaving. (*Beat.*) And I wanted to tell you because I don't think Charlie can keep covering for him at work.

Alice   I see.

Ellen   He's getting old. He won't admit it.

Alice   Right.

Ellen   And when you think about it, I think there are things you could do, aren't there?

Alice   Things I could do?

Ellen   Like getting out of the house. And getting back to work. For, for, for, for Peter as much as for anything.

Alice   It's been very hard.

Ellen   And you could be more.

Alice   What?

Ellen   Doting. To Peter.

Alice   What are you talking about?

Ellen   He's your husband. He needs you. And I've been watching the way that you've been with him and I don't think that it's fair. I'm sorry. I don't. I've been thinking about it a lot.

Alice   Fucking hell.

Ellen   Don't swear. Not at me.

Alice Ellen, I'm sorry that Charlie isn't well. And if he's asked you to tell us so that he didn't have to work because he needed a break, then that's –

Ellen He told me not to tell you. Don't tell him I told you, because he told me not to.

Alice Ellen –

Ellen Peter is my son. You have a responsibility to him now. He's your husband, and that should be where your thoughts are directed.

Alice Are you jealous?

Ellen What?

Alice You are. You're jealous of me.

Ellen Don't be ridiculous.

Alice I never thought.

Ellen If you hurt him –

Alice If I hurt him?! I don't believe this. For fuck's sake!

Ellen I'm trying to help you.

Alice Get out.

Ellen What?

Alice Get out of my house.

Ellen What are you talking about?

Alice Get out. Get out.

Ellen *starts to back away and leave.*

Ellen Alice –

Alice Get out, Ellen. Now. Get out of my house. Get out of my sight.

Ellen *leaves.* **Alice** *watches her go.*

Ten

Outside **Charlie** *and* **Ellen**'s *house. Night time.* **Peter** *confronts* **Ellen** *who is wearing a dressing gown.* **Peter** *is drunk.*

Peter   Why did you talk to her like that?

Ellen   Peter?

Peter   It's nothing to do with you.

Ellen   Peter, it's the middle of the night, you should go home.

Peter   I want to know why you think you can talk to my wife about my family –

Ellen   I wasn't.

Peter   Or about my sons or about my life or about anything.

Ellen   I was worried about you.

Peter   Why, Mum? Why do you think that? Answer me.

Ellen   Are you drunk?

Peter   Oh, piss off!

Ellen   Peter –

Peter   How fucking dare you accuse me of being drunk? Do you have the slightest idea how ironic that is?

Ellen   Don't swear. Not at me.

Peter   When you've sat back and supported and ignored and tolerated and encouraged and nurtured and accompanied, accompanied Dad as he drank his brain into mush and his guts into fuck and his business, Mum, his business into such a pitiful, shitty state that –

Ellen   Peter –

Peter   And you ask me if I'm drunk! For fucksake!

Ellen   Peter, don't.

Peter   Don't what? Don't what, Mum? Come on!

He glares at her. Then turns to leave. She calls after him.

Ellen   I come home and there are four-packs of cider hidden in the cupboard. He thinks I can't find them. This is eleven o'clock in the morning.

Peter   That's completely irrelevant to me.

Ellen   He puts them in the drawer. He thinks he's hiding them from me. He gets up in the middle of the night and I hear him drinking in the bathroom with the light off! He thinks I don't realise! And the way he's been talking. He's been dreadful, Peter. The things he says you wouldn't believe. And if he turned up to work and he was drunk and if he said to a client the kind of things that he says to me –

Peter   Don't you fucking cry on me.

Ellen   Peter, you've no idea.

Peter   Then leave him, Mum. Just go. It's your life. No one's stopping you.

Ellen   What?!

Peter   Look at me, Mum. I have no sympathy for you.

Ellen   Go home.

Peter   I have no sympathy for you and you need to leave us alone.

Ellen   Peter, please go home.

Peter   And I'm going back to work and all. So you can tell Dad he can stay in fucking bed for all I'm concerned. I don't believe he really is ill by the way. Not for one second. And Alice's going back to work. We're all going back to work. 'Cause none of this ever happened. You understand me, Mum? Christopher never died. Alex isn't going. None of this happened here. None of it. Not one bit.

Eleven

The doorway of **Peter** *and* **Alice**'s *house.* **Alex** *and* **Sarah** *are saying goodbye to* **Alice**. *Their bags at their feet.* **Peter** *is waiting to take them.* **Alice** *is still in her dressing gown.*

Alice   Have you packed your socks?

Alex   Course I have.

Alice   It's the one thing people forget sometimes. And have you got a shirt?

Alex   'Have you packed your socks.' Yes, I've got a shirt.

Alice   Is it ironed?

Alex   No. It's not. I'll iron it when I get down there.

Alice   If you're going for job interviews you'll need an ironed shirt, Alex.

Alex   I know, Mum. God. I'm not a –

Alice   And have you got your soap bag?

Alex   Yes, Mum.

Alice   With some soap in it?

Alex   Yes, Mum.

Alice   And some toothpaste?

Alex   Yes.

Alice   And your razor?

Alex   Yes.

Alice   And some shaving foam?

Alex   Yes, Mum. I've got everything. I promise.

Alice   Right. Right. Right. Good. Have you got everything Sarah?

Sarah   Yeah.

Alice   And you've said goodbye to your parents all right?

Sarah Yes. I did. Yeah.

Alice And were they okay?

Sarah They were fine, yeah.

Alice That's good. Yes. Right.

Peter We should be –

Alice I know. All right? I know. I . . . Here.

She looks right into **Alex** *for a while.*

Straightens his T-shirt. Straightens the collar of his jacket. Pats his chest. Smiles at him. Kisses him.

Alex I'll ring you, Mum.

Alice Right.

Alex Tonight.

Alice Right.

Alex I'll be . . .

Alice I know.

Alex I'll see you soon.

Alice Yeah. Yeah. Yes. Yes.

She turns and leaves.

They watch her go.

Twelve

Peter, **Alice**, **Alex** *and* **Sarah** *stand on the platform of Stockport station.*

Some time.

A train arrives.

Sarah Is this it?

Alex   Yeah.

Sarah   Where's our seat?

Alex   B37 and 38.

Peter   Right.

Alex   I'll ring Mum tonight.

Peter   Do.

Alex   I will.

Peter   I know. Look after this one, Sarah, won't you?

Sarah   Course I will.

Peter   He can be a right dozy prat at times.

Sarah   I know.

Peter   And you look after her, you pillock.

Alex   I will, Dad, don't worry.

Peter   And if there are any problems, with money, or with, with, with anything – Just ring me. Won't you?

Alex   Course I will.

Peter   We don't need to tell Mum anything. You can ring me on my mobile if you need to. You know that, don't you?

Alex   I do. I will. I'll be fine. I'm sure, Dad.

Peter   I know. Here.

He takes some money out of his wallet and gives it to **Alex** *who puts it in his back pocket.*

Peter   Take this. Buy yourself a sandwich on the train. Or a beer or something. (*Beat.*) You better be quick. We'll stand here gabbing and the train'll fucking leave. Try telling that to yer Mum.

Alex   Right.

Peter   Bye, Sarah, love.

Sarah   Bye.

Kisses her. Hugs her shoulder.

Peter   Have a safe journey.

Sarah   Thank you, yes. I will. I'll see you soon, I'm sure.

Peter   I'm sure so too.

Sarah   You should come down.

Peter   I will do. Yeah. I'll. (*Pause.*) Here. (*He shakes **Alex**'s hand.*) I'll see you soon, son.

Alex   Yeah.

Peter   Be good.

Alex   Fuck off.

Peter   Look after yourself.

Alex   I will. And you. I'll – (*Beat.*) Bye, Dad.

Alex *and* **Sarah** *leave.*

Peter *watches them go. Stands for some time.*

Part Three

Alice

One

Susan Reynolds' *house.* **Susan Reynolds** *and* **Peter
Holmes**. *Afternoon. August.* **Susan** *is much more noticeably
pregnant.* **Peter** *is applying a chemical wash to her beams. This time
his brush is finer, the work is more delicate. He works without a top
on. She watches him for a bit. She has a drink of juice in her hand.*

Peter It's coming on all right, isn't it?

Susan Yes, it is. I'm really pleased. Thank you.

Peter That's the thing with these houses. They're incredibly
solid. They really knew how to make a house, how to keep
it together.

Susan Yes.

Peter I love some of the buildings, just a little older than
these, where they made them without nails. They made
them with these huge old timbers. You just need to tend the
wood properly and they can withstand the most incredible
conditions.

Susan I love hearing you talk about your work. You're
very lucky. I wish I had a job I felt like that about.

Peter I don't really know about much else. That's the
thing with me.

Susan I wish I had the same enthusiasm. I think
enthusiasm about anything is always infectious.

Peter *continues to work.*

Susan I find my work slightly cut-throat at times. You
spend all this time, you study, you get your A-levels, you go
to university, you spend all these years thinking and you end

up in a job that is basically dependent on your capacity to stab other people in the back.

Beat. He turns to her. Washes his brush in a glass of water.

Peter There must be something about it you love. Otherwise you wouldn't, you'd find something else to –

Susan I don't know. (*Beat.*) I quite like the writers.

Peter Do you?

Susan And occasionally you read something and it makes you change the way you see the world a little bit. And if that happens, which isn't all the time, but is sometimes, then it can feel quite important that you publish it. That you get it out into the . . . so that other people can have the way they see the world changed as well. That's quite good.

He just looks at her now.

Peter Sounds it.

Susan And some of the really great books, some of the most beautiful books, you know nobody's going to buy them. But there are moments within them, or sentences, or characters that stop you from breathing a bit. And you kind of think, well, fuck the money. You know?

Peter *laughs at her swearing. Starts working again.*

Susan I brought you a drink. Here. It's mango juice.

Peter (*grins*) It's what?

Susan Mango juice. (*She sips it before she gives it to him.*) It's lovely.

Peter Right.

He takes it. Drinks it all in one. She watches him drink.

It is lovely. Thank you.

He wipes his mouth with the back of his hand. Passes her the glass back.

Peter   I wish I had an A-level.

Susan   Really?

Peter   Sometimes I think about going back to college. Try and get one.

Susan   It's not too late. You could still do it.

Peter   I don't know where I'd get the time from.

Susan   No.

Peter   I mean even now. Alex, my eldest son, he left home. Did I tell you?

Susan   No.

Peter   Two months ago. He went to live in London.

Susan   Right.

Peter   But I still don't have the time to do the things I want to do. And you finish work and the idea of sitting down to actually read a book or something is just completely exhausting. When there's football on. Or *Big Brother.* Or something. (*Beat.*) I should force myself.

Susan   I know what you mean, though.

Peter   And I do find myself frustrated. Find my brain getting frustrated.

Susan   Well, I do too. Still. After A-levels and university and everything. If that's any consolation.

Beat. She places her hand on his arm.

I'm glad you're back properly. It's good to see you.

Peter   Thank you.

Susan   I did like your dad though.

Peter   Yeah. He can be all right.

Susan   I thought he was nice. He was nice to me.

Peter   That's good.

Susan But it's better having you here. (*Beat.*) I shouldn't have said that.

He smiles at her.

Two

Stockport town centre. **John Robinson** *and* **Alice Holmes**. *She is locking the office of the estate agent where she works. Trying to find the right key.*

John Are you Alice Holmes?

Alice Yes. Yes, I am.

John I've been waiting for you to come back to work. My name's John Robinson.

Alice I know exactly who you are. Please. Leave me alone

John I wanted to see –

Alice I know, about everything. I know that it wasn't your fault. You don't need to explain anything.

John That wasn't what I wanted to do.

Alice I have to lock up. How did you even know I worked here?

John I wanted to –

Alice What?

John When I was a child. When I was at school. To stop myself getting beaten up I developed this remarkable capacity to shrug things off. I've always been able to do it. I can't shrug this off.

Alice Please go now.

John I've tried. I wanted to see you. I wanted to say I'm sorry.

Alice You can't.

John   What?

Alice   It's not enough.

John   No. I know. I'm aware of that. My wife's a woman
called Alison Crane.

Alice   What?

John   When we got married she didn't change her name.
I met her at university. When I was in third year, when we'd
been going out for a year I got her pregnant. And what we
decided to do was have an abortion. I say we, but clearly it
wasn't my, my, my – It changed everything. And although
we had the abortion quite early on in the pregnancy I
remember very clearly at the time thinking that nothing
would ever be the same again because of what we'd done.
And it never was. And this is like that.

Alice   Why are you telling me this?

John   For five years we tried to have another child, but we
were never able to. And we never got over what we'd done,
I think, and we still haven't. And I wanted to see you to tell
you that I am desperately, desperately sorry for what I did
to you. It doesn't matter that it was an accident. It doesn't
matter what the inquest said. None of that matters. I did it.
You know? And I wanted to show you that I'm not a
monster because I thought that might help you.

Alice   How would it?

John   I thought it might allow you a perspective, a
perspective on things, on events, on the situation.

Alice   It won't.

John   I thought there might be some questions that you
wanted to ask me.

Alice   There aren't.

John   I wanted to buy you a coffee.

Alice   No.

John   Or something to eat.

Alice   No. Of course not. Are you mad?

John   I think about him every day. I see his face every day.

Alice   Do you think I don't?

John   I'm sorry. Of course. This was a mistake. This was terrible. I should leave. I'm sorry. I'm –

He pulls out a card from his wallet and tries to pass it to her.

If there's anything, if there's ever, if you have a question or if, I don't know, please, this is my number. Please. Ring me. Or. I'd like to. You know?

Alice (*stares at it*)   Do you expect me to take this?

He folds it into her hand.

John   I just want you to know that I'm offering it to you. I'm sorry. I should go. I'm – Goodbye, Alice.

Three

Peter *and* **Alice**'s *house. Their kitchen. Later that afternoon.*

Peter   You're fucking late.

Alice   Have you been – are you drunk?

Peter   I am a little. I'm sorry. Where have you been?

Alice   I've been to work.

Peter   Right. Of course. Work. Till this time. Which is unusual.

Alice   Peter.

Peter   I had something to tell you. Did you know?

Alice   What?

Peter   Did you hear?

Alice   What?

Peter   I got home from work this afternoon. I thought you might be home. Because you get home before me, was my thinking. But you weren't. (*Beat.*) Mum rang.

Alice   Did she?

Peter   She rang to say that Dad has got, well, it seems that the doctors think that it is possible that Dad has got, that he actually might have cancer. So. They're doing tests. I'm going to go in. And I wanted to tell you. And you weren't here.

Alice   When are you going in?

Peter   Where were you?

Alice   I was working, I told you.

Peter   I don't know whether to believe you or not any more.

Alice   How's Ellen? Does she want me to go round?

Peter   No. Of course she doesn't.

Alice   You can't go and see him in that state.

Peter   I fucking well can, you know? He's my dad, for fuck's sake.

Alice   Calm down.

Peter   What?

Alice   I understand that you're upset.

Peter   Well, that's big of you.

Alice   Do you want me to come with you?

Peter   No. I don't. (*Beat.*) I'm going to go on my own.

Pause.

Alice   Is there anything you want me to do?

Peter   I want you to kiss me. You never kiss me any more.

Pause.

I want you to come over here and to kiss me on my mouth.

She goes over to him.

Kisses him.

It is horribly edgy and tense.

Thank you.

No response.

It was awful, I know.

Four

Stepping Hill Hospital. Later that night. **Charlie** *is asleep in bed.* **Peter** *sits by his bedside.*

Peter   One time. I remember, before you started up on your own, Dad. When you used to work in the mill. If I was poorly or if it was a school holiday and Mum wasn't around, you took us to your work. The first time. I was really excited about it. But when I got there you didn't really know what to do with us. Did you? Just told us to go out into the yard and clear it up for you. I was about ten. I went out there on my own and the yard was full of these big metal crates tied with string and all these boxes had to go into the crates and you took us out there and, I think this is true, you left us there on my own. And I didn't know what to do, Dad. I just stood there. But I remember deciding that I was going to start busting up all these boxes. That was the only thing I could figure out. And squashing them into the crates with all the rest of 'em. And after a bit I'm really getting into it. Smashing the fuck out of them. Watching the men there having their fag breaks. Staring at me. Wondering what the fuck I was doing. And one of them asks us. I tell him I'm with you, with my dad. He asks me what your name is. And I remember being staggered that he had absolutely no idea who you were. And at lunchtime, when you came to find us again, I do remember thinking that there was the smell of booze on your mouth.

Pause.

You so fucking deserve this, you know. You so do.

Pause.

Are you awake? Are you? Dad? Fuck's sake.

Pause.

I watched you with Alex when he was a boy and I'd think it was funny because of how I knew you could really be like. But you were sweet with him. Which was good. But fucking hell.

Pause.

I'd watch you with Christopher. And think, I wish I could do that. Just hold him. Kiss him like that. I'd wish that. Never do that now, eh? Fucked that up. Didn't I?

Pause.

And I do love you. I'm meant to tell you that. I do sometimes. Sometimes I don't.

Pause.

Are you awake? Dad? Dad? Are you awake?

Charlie What?

Peter Dad?

Charlie What?

Peter It's Peter, Dad.

Charlie Right.

Peter You just wake up?

Charlie I think so. Where's your mum?

Peter She's gone home.

Charlie Right.

Peter Alice dropped us off. She took Mum home with her.

Charlie Right.

Peter How you feeling?

Charlie I'm all right. I'm – I could murder a fag.

Peter I don't think you're meant to smoke in here, Dad.

Charlie No. I could just have a crafty one.

Peter *laughs. Looks around him.*

Peter Here. I brought you a present.

Peter *pulls out a plastic bag with six cans of strong cider in them.*

Charlie Right, right, right. I'll put them in the . . .

Peter Okay.

Peter *leaves him the bag.*

Charlie They won't notice. Thanks son, that's smashing.

Peter That's all right. (*Beat.*) You haven't shaved.

Charlie What?

Peter Have you?

Charlie No.

Peter You're growing a bit of a beard. I've never seen you with a beard before.

Charlie I'll shave tomorrow.

Peter It doesn't suit you at all.

Charlie No.

Peter What time you get the results?

Charlie They didn't say.

Peter But it'll be tomorrow?

Charlie   Maybe. Might be the next day.

Peter   You want me to come in for you?

Charlie   No. You're all right. I'll –

Peter   How you feeling about them?

Charlie   A bit. You know?

Peter   Yeah.

A silence.

United won.

Charlie   Yeah. They had it on the telly. I thought they looked all right.

Peter   Yeah, they did.

Charlie   Roy Keane was on form, I thought.

Peter   Yeah. He's had a good season.

Charlie   He's a good player. Stroppy little shit at times, but. He was Sarah's favourite.

Peter   That's right.

Charlie   You heard from them?

Peter   Not for a bit.

Charlie   They doing all right, do you think?

Peter   I think so, Dad, yeah.

Charlie   Do you think he'll come home, ever?

Peter   I don't know.

Charlie   Do you want him to?

Peter   Course I do.

Charlie   And Christopher got the photograph for her. Of Roy Keane. For Sarah.

Peter   The soft bugger.

Charlie   I know. (*Beat.*) What time is it?

Peter   It's late. Visiting's finished. I've been here a while.

Charlie   What have you been doing?

Peter   Nothing. Just sitting here. I read the paper.

Charlie   You should have woken us.

Peter   Yeah. I should have done probably. (*Beat.*) Dad, I should probably get going.

Charlie   Really?

Peter   They'll be wanting us out of here.

Charlie   They've not said.

Peter   I probably should though.

Charlie   Right. Okay. Don't.

Peter   What?

Charlie   Don't go.

Peter   It's late, Dad. I don't want to put them to any bother.

Charlie   Right.

Peter   I'll. I'll. I'll be in tomorrow morning.

Charlie   Right.

Peter   Dad, can I ask you something?

Charlie   You what?

Peter   There's something I want to ask you, can I ask you something?

Charlie   Of course you can.

Peter   Has Mum ever had an affair?

Charlie   Has she what?

Peter   Mum. Has she ever had an affair, do you think?

Charlie God. What a question. No. She hasn't. No, son.
She hasn't. No.

Peter Right.

Charlie Why on earth are you asking me that?

Peter Have you?

Charlie Have I what?

Peter I always wondered if you ever had?

Charlie You what?

Peter I just always thought you had.

Charlie An affair?

Peter Yeah.

Charlie No. Not an – I never. No. I didn't. (*Beat.*) I nearly
did.

Peter What?

Charlie I nearly did, but I didn't. Not properly. There
was a girl in one of the offices. When I was at the mill. And
we, we, one time, we did kiss each other. But that was as far
as it went. It wasn't an affair. I told your mum.

Peter What did she say?

Charlie She asked me if I wanted to leave her. I told her
I didn't. She asked me if I was going to do it again and I
said that I wasn't. She asked me if I was sorry I'd done it.
I told her I wasn't. And she said right, and left the room.

Peter I see.

Charlie It wasn't a big deal. I didn't do it again. I never
really saw her since. (*Pause.*) But I'll tell you. Not a day goes
by when I don't think about her and sometimes it's true that
I'm very, very sorry that I didn't leave Ellen and leave you
and live with her.

A pause.

Peter I don't know what to say.

Charlie No.

Peter Is that why you hit Mum, do you think?

Charlie You what?

Peter Alex told me. Christopher saw you.

Charlie What kind of a – I don't believe you're – I never hit your mother. Not ever.

Peter I don't believe you. I believe Christopher more than I believe you. He makes you look like a liar.

Charlie Peter, I –

Peter I wanted to tell you. I can't be like you any more.

Charlie What are you talking about?

Peter You *know*. I should have told you a long time ago. (*Pause.*) I should be going.

Charlie Don't.

Peter It's late, Dad. I can't wait here.

Five

A café in the centre of Stockport. **John Robinson** *and* **Alice Holmes**. *The next afternoon.* **Alice** *has taken her coat off. The two of them are drinking lattes.*

John I like the element of puzzle about it. I like the purity of mathematics.

Alice Do you?

John There's something truthful about numbers. You don't have an opinion about numbers. They're not subjective. They have this tremendous solidity. In a world where very little actually feels altogether that solid any more. A number is a number.

Beat.

I've not talked about this for years.

She smiles.

Alice   I wish I'd done more at school. I could have done all right. I could have gone to university. We had the family.

Beat.

I'm sorry. Listen to me going on!

John   Don't apologise. You're not going on at all.

She blows on her coffee to cool it. Drinks. Examines his face. He watches her.

Alice   If you could go to one place in the world, where would you go?

John   I don't know.

Alice   Think.

John   I, there is somewhere. No. It doesn't matter. That's silly.

Alice   Where?

John (*drinks*)   Sao Paulo.

Alice   You're lying.

John   I'm not.

Alice   But that isn't where you were going to say.

John   It is, you know.

Alice   I don't believe you.

John   It's true.

Alice   Why?

John   What?

Alice   Why do you want to go to Sao Paolo?

John I like beaches. Football. Brazilians.

Alice Brazilians?

John Thank you for ringing me.

Alice Yes.

John I didn't know if you were going to, or what you would say to me if you did.

Alice No. I'm not entirely sure that I did.

John No.

Alice You remind me of somebody.

John Who?

Alice I can't quite place it. You're very grounded. Aren't you?

John Grounded?

Alice I think you are. Don't worry. I think it's nice.

A long pause.

John It's half-four. God! We've been –

Alice Half-four? Shit.

John I'm sorry.

Alice I've got to –

The two of them stand hurriedly. Finish their coffees. Put on their coats.

John I know. Me too. Please. Let me get this.

He picks up the bill, examines it.

Alice No, really.

John No. Please. I insist. It's been very good. Talking to you. I know that that sounds terribly inappropriate but actually it's true.

Alice   There were all these questions that I wanted to ask you.

John   Of course.

Alice   I'd planned them. In my head. I didn't ask any of them. God! I'm sorry.

John   No, no, no, no that's quite all right.

Beat.

She stands, looks at him straight in the face.

Alice   I'd like to see you again, I think.

Six

Charlie *and* **Ellen**'s *living room.* **Peter** *has taken* **Ellen** *home from the hospital. They are both wearing coats.* **Ellen** *removes hers and hangs it up..*

Peter   I can take you in, in the morning.

Ellen   Thank you.

Peter   If you want me to wait for you, while they get the results, I can be a few hours late for work.

Ellen   That's, maybe – That might be good.

Peter   I should probably go home. See Alice.

Ellen   You could stay a bit. Have a beer. You could ring Alice.

Peter   No. I can't, Mum. I've got to go.

Pause.

Ellen   Have you told Alex about Charlie yet?

Peter   I think Alice was going to ring him.

Ellen   How's he getting on?

Peter   He's well, I think. I think he's having a good time.

Ellen   He's the first of you to leave here. Isn't he? There's something good about that, I think.

Beat.

Peter   I was thinking about Dad.

Ellen   You what, love?

Peter   Tonight. And I was thinking about you and all.
I was thinking all the way home about all of the things that you did for me.

Ellen   You what?

Peter   You take them for granted, don't you? All the times you washed my clothes. Made my tea. Helped me with my homework. Just, generally, just looked after me. Mum. I never realised, you know?

Ellen   Realised what? What's got into you, Peter?

Peter   Nothing. Nothing's got into me. I just wanted to tell you that I was thinking about them and I do realise now and I'm not sorry about what I said to you, 'cause I think I was right to say it, but I do appreciate some things now, as well.

Ellen   Did Charlie say something to you last night, Peter?

Peter   No. No he didn't. He was asleep.

Ellen   Are you all right, love?

Peter   Yeah. I. (*Pause.*) Mum, I think Alice is seeing somebody else.

Seven

John Robinson's *house. The next evening.* **John Robinson**
and **Alice Holmes**. *They are drinking wine. And smoking
cigarettes. She holds hers with an element of discomfort.*

Alice   He used to come into the office. That was where the
account for his yard was held.

John   I see.

He refills their wine glasses.

Alice   So he'd come in every Friday. Which is when I'd
be working, after I finished college. I just ended up chatting
to him. He seemed to always want to come and make his
payments to me. That might just be my imagination, by the
way. And this was what, twenty years ago, and he is a heart-
stoppingly handsome man. He's tall and he's lean and he
has these shoulders. And every week he's coming in and
over the course of a few months the conversation starts
getting more and more flirty. And I love it. I do. It's like
he's flirting without making me feel uncomfortable or
unhappy or –

John   He's making you feel attractive.

Alice   Yes. I think so.

John   It's good when that happens.

Alice   So I ask him out.

John   *You* ask *him* out?

Alice   Yeah. I do. And I think he is a little taken aback.
I mean, I'm just a sixth-former with a weekend job. But he
does say yes. And he takes me to the cinema. He buys us
the tickets. I buy us some fish and chips for our tea on the
way home.

John   That's fair enough, eh?

Alice   I think so. And I kiss him for the first time on our
first date. He has the softest lips which surprises me. For a

man with these – he works with his hands. And the skin on
his hands is hard. But his lips are like – Two nights later
I sleep with him and for me it's the first time. You know?

John I do.

Alice I'm seventeen. We have sex four times and then on
the fifth time what happens is, I think the condom must
have split. And I'm pregnant.

John Jesus.

Alice I don't answer his calls for three days. You know,
I don't know what to do. I go round and see him four days
later and by this stage he's quite surprised to see me. When
I tell him, he's sitting on his bed, this little single bed, with
this duvet, and what he's doing is, he's crying. I dry his eyes
for him. We talk and we decide the sensible thing to do,
because of my A-levels, and because of his work, is for me
to have an abortion. And I leave. And two weeks later he
comes round and tells me not to. That he's been thinking
about it. That he thinks that what he wants to do instead of
me having an abortion is, he wants to ask me to marry him.
Basically. (*Pause.*) And so he does. And I say yes. And we do.
And I leave college. And. I was always going to go back but
then Christopher. (*Pause.*) I've not smoked in six years.

John Shit.

Alice If he finds out, he'll kill me.

John Well, have a Polo.

Alice Yeah.

Beat. She stubs her cigarette out.

He goes to the grave, to Christopher's. All the time.

John Right.

Alice He doesn't think that I know.

John No. Do you, ever?

Alice Yeah, I do, I – Not often. No. I can't bear it.

John   No.

Alice   I didn't like Christopher as much as he did.

John   Don't say that.

Alice   I think that is true.

John   Alice.

Alice   I always preferred Alex. Isn't that a horrible thing to say?

John   It's not, it –

Alice   It is, you know. But it is true as well. I miss him more than I miss Christopher. Things, since he's gone – And sometimes I do think I deserve it. For that reason.

John   You don't.

Alice   No. I know, really. It's just what I think sometimes. I've remembered who it is, by the way. Who you remind me of.

John   Who?

Alice   It's my dad.

Pause.

When you listen, you see, your eyes are very alert. Did you know that?

He looks away from her.

Long pause. She finishes her wine.

What's Alison like?

He refills her glass.

John   She's very tough. She's quite little. She has a lovely nose. She's very independent. She's very intelligent. She wishes she did an MA. She wears beautiful clothes that are often quite dark in colour. I love her very much.

Alice   That sounds –

John   And just one time I sometimes think I'd like to have sex with somebody who isn't my wife. Just to see what it's like. (*Pause.*) That sounded like a pass. Fuck. I didn't mean it to. I wasn't suggesting. Shit. I'm sorry.

Alice (*smiling*)   You probably should be.

John   I am.

Straightening her cutlery, she pushes her plate back.

Alice   Thank you for cooking for me.

John   That's all right. I like to cook. I enjoy it.

Alice   Your house is lovely.

John   Thank you. Alison kind of designed all the, you know, all the things.

Alice   I love all the books.

John   Yeah. I wish I could read them all.

Alice   You said. You should.

John   Maybe I will. (*He puts down his drink. Looks at her.*) Alice, right now, I want more than anything I've ever wanted to kiss your mouth.

Alice   –

John   I'm sorry.

Alice   –

John   I am. I'm really sorry. I'm being stupid. That was awful.

Pause. She pushes her chair back.

Alice   I need to go now. (*Half laughs.*) I don't believe you said that.

John   I'm sorry.

Alice   Can I brush my teeth?

John   What?

Alice (*standing*)   Can I borrow your toothbrush? To brush my teeth. To take the smell of tobacco off them.

John   Yeah. Yes. Of course. It's −

Alice   I know.

She leaves. Comes back in, brushing her teeth.

Stands watching him. Goes back out again.

Comes back. Begins the business of putting her coat on and preparing to leave.

Alice   I want to go now. I'm sorry. I can't −

The two stare at each other for some time.

Eight

Night time. **Alice** *and* **Peter**'s *kitchen.* **Peter** *is watching* Big Brother Live *on the television. He doesn't turn to see* **Alice** *enter. She watches him for a while.*

Alice   I'm going to bed. Are you going to be long?

Peter   No.

Alice   I'll keep your light on.

She goes to leave.

He stays watching the TV.

Peter   Right. (*Beat.*) G'night. (*Beat.*) I love you.

She pauses on her way out.

Alice   Goodnight.

She leaves him watching the television.

Part Four

Peter

One

*Two weeks later. A taxi taking **Sarah** from Stockport station to her mum's house. She is alone with the **Taxi Driver**. She only has one trainer on. The **Taxi Driver** is played by the same actor who played **Christopher**.*

Taxi Driver Whereabouts in Longsight are you going?

Sarah Just off Stockport Road.

Taxi Driver Right.

Pause.

Sarah I lost my trainer.

He checks his rear-view mirror.

Taxi Driver Whereabouts?

Sarah I took it off on the train. I went to sleep so I took my trainers off. I woke up when we got into Stockport and I couldn't find it. I didn't have time to look for it. I feel like a right monghead.

Pause. He checks his rear-view mirror.

Taxi Driver Were you on holiday?

Sarah What?

Taxi Driver In London. Were you down on holiday?

Sarah No. I – I was kind of living there for a while.

Taxi Driver Right.

Pause. He checks his rear-view mirror.

How long were you down for?

Sarah   Six months.

Taxi Driver   I've never been.

Sarah   You're not missing much.

Taxi Driver   No?

Sarah   It's horrible.

Taxi Driver   Right. Were you working down there?

Sarah   For a bit. I was living with my boyfriend.

Pause. He checks his rear-view mirror.

Taxi Driver   He still down there, is he?

Sarah   Yeah. I think so. I don't know. I don't care. He's an arsehole.

Taxi Driver   I see.

Sarah   Well. Not an arsehole. He's a coward. He doesn't know what he wants. He's a bit fucked up. You know what I mean?

Taxi Driver   I do, yeah.

Pause. He checks his rear-view mirror.

Does he know you've come back?

Sarah   No.

Taxi Driver   Did you not tell him?

Sarah   No. I didn't.

Pause.

Taxi Driver   He might get worried, you know?

Sarah   Don't care. Dickhead. He deserves to get worried.

Pause. He checks his rear-view mirror.

Taxi Driver   I'm not being rude or anything, sweetheart, and I know it's not any of my business, but I think you should tell him.

Sarah What?

Taxi Driver I think you should.

Sarah Do you?

Taxi Driver It's really difficult, isn't it?

Sarah What is?

Taxi Driver Just, the whole business of, you know, being very complicated.

Pause.

Sarah Are you a bit mental?

Taxi Driver I think you should call him.

Sarah You don't know what you're talking about.

Taxi Driver I bet you do and all. I bet you.

Two

Next evening. **Alice** *and* **Peter***'s kitchen.* **Alice** *is with* **Alex***, who has just returned. They've been talking a while but his bag and his coat are still at his feet. They're both drinking: she wine, he a small bottle of beer.*

Alice When did she leave?

Alex Two days ago.

Alice Does she know you're back?

Alex No.

Alice You should tell her, Alex.

Alex I know.

Alice I'm really sorry – about Paul, and everything.

Alex It was frightening.

Alice Is he gonna be all right?

Alex   I don't think he is, Mum, no.

Alice   If you want to go and see him. Go and visit. When you find out what's happening or where he is then you can do, you know. We could take you.

Alex   I'll be all right. I think you two have got enough to worry about at the moment, haven't you?

Alice   It's –

Alex   What are you gonna do, Mum?

Alice   I wish Dad was alive. He'd know what to do.

Alex   He isn't, though.

Alice   No.

Alex   You should talk to him, to Dad, you know?

Alice   Listen to you.

Alex   What?

Alice   Giving me advice. All grown up. He doesn't deserve you sticking up for him, you know?

Alex   He does, I think

Alice   You've no idea.

Alex   I do, you know.

Alice   I'm glad you're back.

Alex   Yeah.

Alice   Don't ever leave my sight. Will you? Always stay where I can see you, Alex. Always.

Alex   Mum, you're being ridiculous.

Alice   You could buy a shirt, though.

Alex   A what?

She touches his T-shirt under his coat. Examines it, slight joking distaste.

Alice   A shirt. You could do. I'd give you the money.

Alex *laughs*.

Alice   I'm just saying.

Alex   I'm going to go and see Christopher.

Alice   Right.

Alex   Do you go, ever?

Alice   Of course I do.

Alex (*drinks first*)   You don't though, do you?

Alice (*drinks too*)   I go more than you do.

Alex   Yeah.

Alice (*puts her drink down*)   He loved you like mad, you know?

Alex   I know he did. (*He can't speak for a second.*) Soft bugger. He used to right do my head in.

Alice   I know. He did everybody's head in.

Three

Susan Reynolds' *house.* **Peter Holmes** *is being paid by her. She is very heavily pregnant now. Late afternoon.*

Susan   It looks lovely, in this light, doesn't it?

Peter   Yeah. It's good. It's a good colour.

Susan   And it'll last.

Peter   Yeah. It'll outlive us two.

Susan   That's rather extraordinary to me.

Pause.

'On the shore of the wide world I stand alone, and think,
Till Love and Fame to nothingness do sink.'

Peter   What's that?

Susan   Sorry, it's just a. It's a poem. A sonnet. By John Keats. (*Beat. He looks at her.*) It's one of my favourites. Here. Let me. Is a cheque all right?

Peter   Yeah. That's great. That's perfect. Thank you.

Susan   No. Thank you. What are you going to spend it on?

Peter   I don't know.

Susan   You should buy your wife a present.

Peter   You reckon?

Susan   Yes. I think you should.

Peter   You don't know my wife.

Susan   Hmm.

She writes and hands him a cheque.

Peter   Good luck with the, with the baby and everything.

Susan   Thank you.

Peter   How long have you got now?

Susan   Two weeks.

Peter   Could be any day then.

Susan   Don't say that.

Peter   It could be, though.

Susan   Yeah. I know.

Peter   It'll be all right, you know?

Susan   You think so?

Peter   It will. House like this. All you need i'n't it?

Susan   I don't know. I think, maybe. (*Pause.*) It's still bright.

Peter   Yeah.

Susan This time of day.

Peter Yeah.

Susan Thank you. For all your work and your company and for, for, for everything.

Peter That's my pleasure.

Susan I don't think I've met anybody quite like you, you know? Before. (*Beat.*) I'm very pleased. (*Beat.*) With all this.

Peter I'm glad.

Susan I feel like I ought to send you a photograph or let you know when it's born. Or. Something. Or –

Peter Yeah.

Susan I won't. Don't worry.

Peter No.

Susan I wonder what she's like, your wife?

Peter I –

Susan I bet she's very strong, isn't she?

Peter Strong?

Susan I bet she's really lovely. She's very lucky. I'm sorry. I'm being embarrassing now.

Peter No you're not.

Susan I should be –

Peter You were the first person I told, you know? The first person I told the story to. About Christopher. That means I won't ever forget you.

Pause.

I don't know anybody else who knows poems. Off by heart.

Four

The Bluebell Hotel. **Alex** *meets* **Sarah** *there. She is wearing her glasses. He is drinking a can of beer.*

Sarah   I came because I wanted an apology.

Alex   Right.

Sarah   Because you owed me one.

Alex   I know.

Sarah   So apologise.

Alex   I'm sorry.

Sarah   That sounded fucking sincere I must say.

Alex   Sarah –

Sarah   Don't. All right? Just don't.

He finds another can of beer from the bag at his feet. Opens it and passes it to **Sarah**.

Alex   Mum and Dad are gonna split up.

Sarah   Are they?

Alex   I hope so.

Sarah   Why?

Alex   'Cause he's doing her head in and she had an affair.

Sarah   Did she?

Alex   Not really.

Sarah   Fucking hell.

Alex   And Paul's gonna get sent to prison or to hospital or something. Probably.

Sarah   Good. He deserves it.

Alex   So that's my news, what's yours?

Sarah   Fuck off.

She reaches into her bag. Pulls out a vial of pills. Takes one. Swallows it without water.

Alex   I thought you'd stopped taking those.

Sarah   Well, I haven't. I wish I could. It does my head in.

Pause. She washes it down with a mouthful of beer.

Alex   Sarah. I'm really sorry.

Sarah   I know.

Alex   It was horrible. I was horrible. I behaved like a wanker. I was horrible to you. I'm very ashamed of myself.

Sarah   You should be.

Alex   I am. Honestly.

Sarah   Good. That's good, then. Don't go on about it.

She turns her back to him to replace her pills in her bag.

Alex   I'm really glad you came.

Sarah   I know.

Alex   I didn't think you would. The way you sounded on the phone.

Sarah   I was fucking furious with you, that's why. You behaved like a complete wanker.

Alex   I know.

Pause.

She moves away from him. Looks around the hotel.

Sarah   What do you want to do?

Alex   What?

Sarah   Here.

Alex   I wanted to spend the night here.

Sarah   The night?

Alex   Yeah.

Sarah   All night?

Alex   Yeah, I think so.

Sarah   Fucking hell.

Alex   What?

Sarah   It'll be freezing. Middle of the night. You'll never get to sleep.

Alex   It's summer. It's not that cold.

Beat.

Sarah   It's odd, coming here.

Alex   Yeah. (*Beat.*) I went to the grave today. I should have gone there more often.

Sarah   You should have done.

Alex   But here's better. Makes me think about him more. I like spending the night in strange places. It's like camping. I wanted to, tonight.

Sarah (*finishes her beer*)   There's things we all want to do, Alex. We just can't always do them, you know what I mean? (*About the beer.*) That was the last one.

Alex (*offers her his beer*)   Want some of mine?

Sarah   No thank you.

Alex   You want my jacket?

Sarah   Yes please.

She puts his jacket on.

Alex   What kind of things would you like to do? That you might not be able to.

Pause before she answers.

Sarah   Give up all my pills. (*Beat.*) Leave home. (*Beat.*) Do it properly though. Not go and crash on your wanker-psycho mate's floor.

Alex   Yeah.

Sarah   Live until I'm twenty-five, at least.

Alex   You what?

Sarah   You heard.

Alex   You'll do that.

Sarah   I hope so.

Pause.

I'm sorry about your mum and dad.

Alex   Yeah.

Sarah   Marriage is odd.

Alex   Yeah.

Sarah   Sometimes I think it's a completely insane idea.

He looks at her.

Alex   You never fancy it?

She looks back straight at him.

Sarah   Sometimes.

Alex   Really?

Sarah (*grinning*)   I'd marry Roy Keane.

Alex   Fuck off.

Sarah   He's gorgeous.

Alex   He's fucking hanging. Fucking thick and all.

Sarah   He is not. He's just got a very particular type of intelligence.

Alex   Yeah. The thick type. (*Pause.*) Nobody else?

Sarah   You what?

Alex   Would you never marry anybody else?

Sarah *smiles. Looks away from him.*

Some time.

Sarah My mum and dad's marriage is fucking weird and all.

Alex You're telling me.

Sarah They were nearly all right, you know?

Alex You what?

Sarah And then, just at the last minute, they fucking lost the plot.

Alex Are you crying?

Sarah No.

Alex Don't cry.

Sarah I'm not.

Pause.

He positions her in his eye-line and draws a line around her with his finger.

What are you doing?

Alex I'm drawing a line around you. With my finger.

Five

Charlie *and* **Ellen***'s back yard.* **Alex** *has gone looking for* **Charlie***.* **Charlie** *is drinking a beer. The next morning.*

Charlie What's happened to you? You look like you slept in a ditch.

Alex I didn't.

Charlie Good. I should hope not.

Alex Is Gran in?

Charlie No, mate, she's not.

Alex   That's good.

Charlie   Why?

Alex   I didn't want to see her. I wanted to see you.

Charlie   Right. That's good. Sit down, mate. How are yer?

Alex   I'm all right, thank you. How are you?

Charlie   I'm fine. I'm good. I'm all right.

Alex   I heard about you lying about getting cancer.

Charlie   You what? I wasn't lying! God!

Beat. **Alex** *grins. He doesn't sit down. So* **Charlie** *stays standing too.*

Charlie   The doctors thought. There were tests. I was clear. I wasn't lying.

No response. **Alex** *pulls out a packet of cigarettes.* **Charlie** *watches him.* **Alex** *lights one. Grins at his Grandad.*

Alex   You're not having one.

Charlie *smiles and deflates a little. Watches* **Alex** *smoke.*

Charlie   Your gran said you got back yesterday.

Alex   That's right.

Charlie   How was London?

Alex   It was fucking terrible.

Charlie   Right. Good. I could've told you that, you know. I heard about your spot of bother.

Alex   Spot of bother?

Charlie   Your dad told us. I was sorry to hear that.

Alex   It was hardly a spot of bother, Grandad. My best mate's gonna get sent to prison for burning a house down.

Charlie   Yes.

Alex   That's not really a spot of fucking bother, Grandad, is it?

Pause. **Charlie** *drinks, smiles at him.*

Charlie   I've not been to London for years. I always hated it.

Alex   I'm not surprised.

Pause.

Charlie   How was the train journey?

Alex   The what?

Charlie   That's the best thing about it, I think. The train journey. Sit on the train. See the whole country. All of it. Spread out.

Alex   Grandad, Christopher told me that he saw you batter Gran.

Charlie   What?

Alex   I never told you that I knew but one of the things I decided I was going to do when I came back was tell you that I found out.

Charlie   Right.

Alex   And you should know that that was one of the reasons that I left.

Charlie   Right.

Alex   You fucking bastard coward.

Pause.

Charlie   Do you want a beer?

No response.

Do you?

Alex   No.

Charlie I'm having a beer, are you sure you don't want one? Have a beer outside in the sunshine. Sorts things out a bit.

Alex I don't think so.

Charlie Go on, mate, have a beer. Here. Have it.

Charlie *opens two cans of beer and passes an opened one to* **Alex**, *who takes it.*

Very long pause as they drink their beer without looking at each other.

Charlie Is that better?

Alex What?

Charlie For having said it out loud?

No response.

I thought it would be.

Pause.

I'm not only that, you know. I'm not saying you're wrong. I'm saying I am sometimes. But sometimes I'm actually not.

Long silence.

I never knew what my dad did in the war. And I never asked him. But when he came back, he kind of, it was like, he carried it around with him. He only came to live with us when I was seven. I was seven years old. Never even knew the fucker. He comes home. Sits in his chair. He used to – he had this plank. This plank of wood. And if he were . . . Sometimes you just knew. The way he was looking at yer. The way, sometimes it was like, it was just the way he was breathing. Knew you were gonna get one. Get it on your legs. Yer arse.

Pause.

I never even met a girl until I were fourteen. Wanted to go to your school. That was around when I was your age. Go to Stockport School. But I couldn't get in. I never passed the exams.

Pause.

I was in Dresden. When I met Ellen. She was working as a nurse on attachment there. I was with the Engineers. Doing my National Service. I hated it. Hated the whole – The routine of it. And the tension. I never met any single person who I thought was real or who I actually liked. There's all this front. People pretending. They put it all on.

Pause.

I'm twenty-one and I turn the radio on and it's this voice.

> 'Well, since my baby left me
> I found a new place to dwell,
> It's down at the end of Lonely Street
> At Heartbreak Hotel.'

Pause.

Your gran wanted to sell the house. She asked me to look into how much money we'd get. To ask yer mum. I didn't. I spoke to somebody else. A bloke I know from Winter's. When yer gran was out, he sent an Estate Agent round. He said he'd put it on the market at £180,000. We bought it for five thousand. I haven't told her. She's not asked me yet. If I tell her, she'll definitely want to go.

Pause.

You have no right to call me a coward. Nobody has any right to call another person a coward. We're all of us cowards. All of us.

Alex   I used to think you were a proper man, you know? I used to think the way you loved Gran was amazing. It was incredible to me. When I heard that you did that –

Beat.

I was gonna tell her she should leave you.

Charlie   Were you?

Alex   I don't know if I think she should or not any more. But I was really going to.

Charlie Right.

Alex Are you gonna tell me I know nothing now?

Pause.

Charlie I'll tell you something. Peter is a much, much better dad to you than I was to him. And if you ever have a kid I bet you a thousand pounds that you'll be a better dad to your kid than Peter is to you. But I was a better dad to Peter than my dad was to me. You might say I couldn't have been any worse. But even so. It counts.

Alex You reckon?

Charlie It does.

Alex I'm not sure.

Six

Charlie *and* **Ellen***'s living room.* **Charlie** *and* **Ellen** *look out of their window. Later that day. He drinking beer, she drinking vodka and tonic.* **Ellen** *can't look at* **Charlie** *throughout this whole scene, however hard he tries to get her to.*

Charlie If we went back. Let's not go to where the barracks were. I'd love to go into the mountains. Or where the forests were. All that time and we never saw them. I was thinking that I'd like to do that. Would you like to do that, Ellen, do you think?

Ellen I'm not sure. It's never really crossed my mind.

Charlie And I was thinking. Maybe this weekend. We could go into town and get on a bus, or a train, we could go to Nottingham. Go back to Nottingham. You could show me round.

Ellen I don't know anywhere in Nottingham any more.

Charlie Or we could just go walking. Could get in the car and go out to Dunham Massey. Go out to Lyme Park. Or Buxton. Or Edale. Just have a walk. Couldn't we?

Ellen   I don't know.

Charlie   Or just go on a stroll. Go out. Stroll around. Go down to the Bluebell.

Ellen   It's closed. It's been closed years.

Charlie   I know. I still think about it, though. I still remember going seeing you.

Ellen   Charlie.

Charlie   We could go down to the Crown, then. Have a beer. Come on, Ellen.

Ellen   Don't.

Charlie   What?

Ellen   Just. (*Pause.*) Did you see Alex?

Charlie   Yeah. You missed him.

Ellen   How was he?

Charlie   He was all right. It was good to see him.

Ellen   I should go over.

Charlie   They're having a roast. On Sunday. Alex invited us over.

Ellen   Right. Good. That'll be nice. It's good to have him back.

Charlie   I think so.

Ellen   I saw Angus Morsten's wife when I was out.

Charlie   Really?

Ellen   It'll be a year. Soon.

Charlie   Yeah.

Ellen   She's looking terrible. Really. Like she's carrying this, this, this, weight.

Charlie   I've not even seen her.

Ellen It got me thinking all kinds of things, you know?

Charlie Really?

Ellen I've only ever made love to you. In my whole life. Did you know that?

Charlie –

Ellen And I've often thought about what it would be like. The shape of other men's bodies. How they fit. The way they feel. (*Long pause.*) Did you ever find out how much the house would cost?

Charlie No. No. I didn't. No.

Ellen Will you?

Charlie Yes.

Ellen 'Cause I can.

Charlie No, I'll do it.

Ellen You say that.

Pause. They look out of the window.

Seven

The bridge over the motorway. **Alex** *and* **Peter** *look down, watching the cars.*

Peter You wanna go to County later?

Alex You what?

Peter It was just a question.

Alex Fucking hell, Dad.

Peter They're playing.

Alex Right.

Peter Burnley.

Alex   Right.

Peter   Local derby.

Alex   Right.

Peter   I've not been for ages. I was wondering if you wanted to go.

Alex   No, thank you.

Peter   Two of us. Watch it together and that. Go and have a fight. Kick off. Father and son. Against Burnley. Be easy, that.

Alex   Have you gone completely insane?

Peter   I used to, you know.

Alex   Fuck off.

Peter   I did. Just after you were born. I never told yer mum. Used to be good fun and all. I miss it sometimes. Your fault that.

Alex   What?

Peter   It is. Buggerlugs. If you hadn't come along I'd still be down there.

Alex   Sorry. Not. (*Pause.*) I went to see Grandad.

Peter   How was he?

Alex   He was pissed. It was only eleven o'clock and all.

Peter   Right.

Alex   Has he stopped smoking now?

Peter   I think so. It's hard to tell. He hides things.

Alex   Yeah. Did they find out what was the matter with him?

Peter   Not properly. He thinks he's got off because the cancer scan was clear. But . . . They've been a bit rubbish, as it goes.

Pause.

Alex He's not as daft as he makes out, is he?

Peter No.

Alex I quite like that about him. He was a fucker to Gran, though.

Peter You're funny.

Alex Why?

Peter You're like all the good bits of me with none of my rubbish bits.

Alex What are your rubbish bits?

Peter I never *do* anything. I should.

Alex Why do you think that is? What kind of things would you want to do?

Peter Play for County.

Alex I wish you'd fucking shut up about them! It's a bit embarrassing! County are shite. Man U I could understand but fucking County! Anyway. I'm being serious.

Peter I want to buy a bigger yard.

Alex Well, you should then.

Peter I know.

Alex Go and get a loan. You'd get it, I reckon.

Peter I know.

Alex Well then.

Peter I know.

Alex You won't though, will you? God!

Peter I want to take your mum away somewhere.

Alex Where?

Peter   She always wanted to go orange-picking. In Spain.
I always thought I'd take her. Surprise her.

Alex   Well, you should.

Peter   And I want to ask you to stay.

Alex   Right.

Peter   And not go again. Not for a while.

Alex   Right.

Peter   I want to do that and all. But I don't think I dare.

A long pause. They watch the cars. **Alex** *lights a cigarette.*

Alex   You know I can't don't you? It'd be, it'd be, it would
be impossible, Dad.

Peter   I know.

Alex   I'd hate it.

Peter   Yeah.

Alex   I'm not being impolite.

Peter   No. I know.

Alex   I'm sorry.

Eight

Alice *and* **Peter**'s *kitchen.* **Sarah** *is waiting for them to come back
to go out with* **Alex**.

Alice   I like you.

Sarah   You what?

Alice   I think you're a lot stronger than you make out.
That's one of my favourite qualities in anybody. But
especially in a woman.

Sarah   Thank you.

Alice But this is my kitchen.

Sarah Right.

Alice I don't mind you using it. But you ask me.

Sarah I –

Alice You understand?

Sarah Yes.

Alice You better.

Sarah I do.

Alice *smiles at her.* **Sarah** *smiles back.*

Nine

A hillside in Buxton. **Alice** *and* **Peter** *have gone for a drive and have left their car and are lying on the ground near to it.*

Peter I was going to lock the doors.

Alice You what?

Peter I was going to. I was going to put a tube in the exhaust and turn it on and stick it in the windows and lock the doors and have the two of us sit there.

Alice Fucking hell, Peter.

Peter It's all right, you know.

Alice You what?

Peter I didn't.

Alice Peter.

Peter I figured it out.

Alice You what?

Peter I figured it out. I know. About you and, and, and . . . Well. I don't know who. But I know that you've fallen in

love with somebody else. That you've been lying to me
about where you've been going. That you've been going out
and, and, and dressing up and going out and I don't know,
fucking, have you been? You've been fucking some other guy.
I know that. Don't try and deny it, Alice, because I know it.

Alice   I haven't.

Peter   I said don't try and deny it, Alice.

Alice   I haven't though, Peter. It's not true.

Peter   You don't even need to look at me. I can tell. When
I saw you. Way you were dressed. I knew then. Because
you're not dressing like that for me, are you, Alice? Are you
though mate?

Alice   I've not been doing anything.

Peter   Part of me doesn't even mind. Part of me reckons
it's good. Good that you, you know. That there's somebody
you felt for.

Alice   I've not done anything.

Peter   And part of me wants to get the cunt's face and
grind it into the pavement.

Alice   There isn't a cunt. There's not a – You're wrong.
I didn't do anything.

Peter   Liar.

Alice   I nearly did. I didn't.

Peter   What?

Alice   I nearly did. And then I didn't.

Peter   What do you mean by that?

Alice   I mean exactly what I said. There was an opportunity.
And I didn't take it.

Peter   An opportunity?

Alice   A friend, a man you don't know, somebody from
work, a man who occasionally I have met outside of work

for, for, for coffee or to drink or to chat or, one time, he, he
wanted to, he tried to. I didn't do anything. There was part
of me that wanted to. But I didn't.

Peter   Right.

Alice   And you always say that and it does my head in.
I was standing looking at this, this, this, this man, at this
man and he wanted so badly to kiss me, to touch me, just
to have me. And he's a handsome man. And he's interesting
and he's alive and he's funny and he, he does things. He
does. He – But I did nothing. Because of you. So don't
speak to me as though it would be perfectly within your
rights to put a tube in our exhaust pipe, you fucking, you
wanker idiot coward. I did nothing. I didn't.

*There is a very long pause. The two of them have nowhere to go from
here.*

Peter   He didn't die straight off. Christopher.

Alice   Don't.

Peter   I wanted to tell you. I've been carrying it around.
I held his head and his eyes kind of flickered.

Alice   I don't want to know this.

Peter   His breathing was all jagged. And it did look, it did
look like it was just horrible. It wasn't peaceful. It wasn't
sudden. It hurt him I think. I wanted you to know that
because every time I open my eyes I see him hit and every
time I close them I see him dying.

Pause.

And I blame the pub. And I blame the landlord. And I blame
the brewery and I blame the people who made the chairs
there and the television. And I blame the people who grew
the barley and distilled the water and made the crates and
the kegs and the van drivers who drove it there. Because if
one of them had decided not to then maybe I wouldn't have
gone. Maybe I wouldn't have done. Maybe I'd have gone
with him instead. And maybe we'd still have him. But that's

just insane talk, that. I know that. I know. And I know that
really it should have been me who should have stopped him,
I know that it was nobody else's fault but mine. I know that.
And I'm sorry, Alice. But there's nothing I can do about it
now. I feel sick all of the time.

Alice   That means nothing to me.

Peter   No. (*Pause.*) You know how many stars there are up
there? In the Milky Way?

Alice   No.

Peter   Two hundred billion. Sometimes. Night like this.
You lie back. You start to see properly. See more and more
of 'em. I used to like it. Makes me want to die now. Makes
me want to vomit. I don't sleep. I'm tired all the time but
my dreams scare the shit out of me

Pause.

I wish he hadn't died, Alice.

Alice   I know. I do too.

Peter   I still love you, you know? I can't stop myself. I wish
I could sometimes. I look at you and it stops my heart. And
I know that you don't love me any more. But for once I
wanted to do something. For once I wanted to – I still love
you. I still love you and, God, I don't want you to leave me,
Alice. I don't want you to go. I'd – I'd – I'd –

Alice   Don't.

*She puts a finger to his lips. Very long pause. They look at each other.
She moves her finger away.*

I didn't do anything. How could I do anything to you?

Peter   We should get back. It'll be cold. The roads and
that.

Alice   Peter. Wait.

Peter   What?

Alice   Can I lie on you?

Peter   What?

Alice   Can I lie my head on you? Can we wait here for a bit and I'll lie my head on you?

He looks at her.

There is some time.

He lies down on his back.

She moves over, lies curled up into a ball, with her head on his chest.

He strokes her hair.

Ten

Peter *and* **Alice***'s house.* **Alice***,* **Sarah** *and* **Ellen** *are preparing the roast dinner.* **Alice** *is maybe offstage, but certainly removed from the physical heart of the action − an area which is dominated, for the first time, by a large dining table.* **Charlie** *is sitting by the table drinking.* **Alex** *is sitting with him but not drinking.* **Peter** *is setting the table. Putting an undercloth and then a tablecloth on it. Place mats. Wine bottles. Cutlery, etc.*

Sarah   The sprouts are ready.

Alice   Great.

Sarah   And the carrots. And the cauliflower. And the peas.

Alice   Great.

Alex   I fucking hate cauliflower.

Sarah   Alex, don't swear. You don't have to have it.

Ellen   She's right, Alex.

Alex   I was just saying.

Sarah   Well, just don't.

Ellen   How's the gravy, Alice?

Alice   Getting there.

Charlie   I love the smell of gravy.

Peter   You awake, Dad?

Charlie   Don't you?

Peter   How long you been awake for?

Charlie   Sunday afternoon. Bit of footy on the telly. Couple of pints.

Alex   A couple?!

Charlie   Back home in plenty of time for the roast and the veg and the gravy. Fantastic that.

Ellen   And meanwhile Alice is here working all afternoon in the kitchen so that you can watch your football and drink your –

Alex   She likes it.

Ellen   That doesn't matter.

Alex   Don't you Mum?

Alice   Don't I what?

Alex   Don't you like cooking for everybody? Making us all our tea?

Alice   I love it, Alex. I could think of nothing I'd rather be doing with my time. Not one thing. Not anything ever.

Alex   Told you.

Sarah   She's being sarcastic, monghead.

Alex   She isn't. She's being serious. Aren't you, Mum? Aren't you being serious?

Alice   Is that table laid yet?

Sarah   No.

Alex   I'm doing it!

Sarah   You give them one job!

Alex   Shut it. Grass.

Sarah   It's true though. One job.

Peter   That smells amazing, Alice.

Alice   Thank you.

Peter   Not had a, a, a roast for a long time, I don't think.

Alice   No.

Peter   It smells fantastic.

Charlie   Can I have another beer please, Peter?

Peter   We're about to eat, Dad.

Charlie   Well, I'll bring it with me then, to sit down. I can actually eat and drink at the same time, you know.

Peter   Alex, mate, get your grandad a beer, would you, love?

Alex   He can get himself a beer, can't he?

Peter   Alex.

Sarah   He's bone-idle sometimes, that son of yours, you know?

Peter   I know.

Alex   I'm going. Shut it, you.

Sarah   Bone idle.

Alex *goes to fetch a beer.*

Alice   Could you open a bottle of wine please, love?

Peter   I have done. I opened two. One red and one white.

Alice   Thanks sweetheart.

Peter   Do you want a glass?

Alice   What?

Peter   Do you want a glass of wine, Alice?

Alice   No, no. No. No, I'm fine. I'll wait. I'll – Just lay the table, will you?

Peter   Course.

Alice   Ellen, Sarah, could you – ? I'm, just taking the chicken out. Could you come and – ?

Sarah   Course.

Ellen   Course we can, love. Peter's right, it does smell amazing, you know?

Ellen *and* **Sarah** *leave to join* **Alice**. *They leave.* **Alex** *returns with the beer.*

Peter, **Alex** *and* **Charlie** *are left alone,* **Peter** *and* **Alex** *setting the table.*

Alex   Here's your beer, Grandad.

Charlie   Thank you.

Alex   I poured it like a bit of a spastic, I'm afraid. The head's fucked.

Charlie   Right.

Peter   Alex, could you get the place-mats out?

Alex   Sure.

Peter   Dad, could you get the knives out for me?

Charlie   Sorry?

Peter   The knives, out of the drawer. Could you get them out for me?

Charlie   Of course I can.

He stands to collect the knives. Gets them. Starts distributing them. His movements are painfully slow. **Alex** *and* **Peter** *do notice this. They don't say anything.*

Here we are.

Peter   Thank you. Thanks, Dad. Just put them there. Thank you.

The men continue to set the table for a while.

Lights fade.